Fi-Fa's, Levys and the Collection of Judgments in Georgia

by
Rickey E. Tumlin

Bloomington, IN Milton Keynes, UK

authorHOUSE™

AuthorHouse™
1663 Liberty Drive, Suite 200
Bloomington, IN 47403
www.authorhouse.com
Phone: 1-800-839-8640

AuthorHouse™ UK Ltd.
500 Avebury Boulevard
Central Milton Keynes, MK9 2BE
www.authorhouse.co.uk
Phone: 08001974150

First published by AuthorHouse 02/27/2006

ISBN: 1-4259-1177-3 (sc)

Library of Congress Control Number: 2006920722

Printed in the United States of America
Bloomington, Indiana

This book is printed on acid-free paper.

ACKNOWLEDGEMENT

The author would like to express his appreciation to former Captain Buddy M. Waldrep, Hall County Sheriff's Office Retired, without whose personal knowledge, patience and guidance, the author would never have gained the knowledge and training culminated in this work. The author would like to further thank everyone concerned for their efforts involved in the production of related information from which the author has been trained over the course of his career. Also, to Mr. Paul Stanley and Mr. Benjamin Bagwell, attorneys at law, whose assistance in reviewing the material for the legal cites is most deeply appreciated.

An invitation for future collaboration on revisions and updates is extended to anyone experienced in the field able to extend the availability of knowledge and expertise. The author is willing to collaborate with anyone wishing to increase the range of the information contained within, to the betterment of all concerned.

Dedicated to all law enforcement
professionals
responsible for the execution of writs
and the performance of levys.

DISCLAIMER

The author has generated this publication in an effort to provide a reference source of accurate and authoritative information concerning the collection of judgments. The author is not an attorney and does not pretend to have all inclusive nor comprehensive knowledge of the subject matter. The author is not engaging in the practice of providing legal advice.

The information contained in this publication is not intended to replace the services of an attorney. However, it is designed and intended to provide introductory familiarization with tools and methods of collection otherwise not immediately available to the public. This compilation is derived from the author's research, combined with many years of training and experience in this field.

It is hoped that the information provided in this volume will become a ready resource for the uninitiated in the collection of judgments. If legal advice or any other expert advice is required, you should seek the services of a competent attorney or other professional.

The information contained in this volume is believed to be accurate and up to date, but not guaranteed to have all the latest decisions. Any person or entity, which relies on information obtained solely from this publication, does so at his or her own risk. The author assumes no liability for actions taken by persons relying solely on the information contained herein.

Policies and procedures vary from state to state. Although all the states rely on old English common law and a lot of states have had similar issues settled by case law, it would be best not to rely solely on information obtained from this publication in executing a levy in states other than Georgia. Even though a goodly portion of this information is generic and could be applied from one state to another, it would be advisable to consult your county attorney before attempting to execute a levy and seizure in a state other than Georgia, using these guidelines. Additional and separate research should be conducted first.

The author claims no responsibility for any mistakes in spelling, grammar, or typesetting involved in the printing and manufacture of this publication. All rights are reserved for the reproduction of this material contained herein. Certain pronouns have been used to encompass the corporate, gender-based and plural defendants. These pronouns may appear to be grammatically incorrect, but are used to convey a generic message.

INTRODUCTION

No matter how successful the efforts in obtaining the judgment, it is useless if you are unable to collect it. The author has tried to provide practical and clear information in an effort to eliminate wasted time, effort and expense. This work is intended to enable the judgment plaintiff to access resources that may facilitate rapid and successful collection of the judgment. Though much of the laws, decisions and practices exist in other states, this is written and compiled from the perspective of the collection of judgments in Georgia.

The need has arisen for a readily available resource of information for the collection of judgments styled and written for the layperson. Attorneys have ready access to their law libraries and consultation with fellow practitioners. Professional collection agencies have the advantage of years of experience and the resource of their company attorney. Some reference is made to decisions based on policy established by the Hall County Sheriff's Office over the author's years of employment and may not be totally acceptable by other jurisdictions. Any question on this issue should be referred to your department head, local county attorney, or the issuing judges.

By publication of this work, it has been the author's aim to facilitate the timely and uneventful, but successful collection of judgments. To be as beneficial as possible, the author has attempted to encompass as much as possible the experience gained through his more than thirty-two years with the Hall County Sheriff's Office. Any redundancy has been intentional to emphasize caution and safety, or where the redundancy occurs to clarify a separate phase or act.

The task of successfully collecting a judgment can be very arduous. It can be highly time consuming and even taxing on your financial resources. In some cases even the most diligent of efforts are not rewarded. It is a very fulfilling and rewarding endeavor, to achieve the successful collection of a judgment.

It is hoped that this book provides sufficient hints, clues and suggestions to assist the judgment plaintiff and the levying officer in their efforts. No prudent individual will set out to fail. It is the hope of the author to be of assistance by providing some leads in the seeking out of the information required to successfully collect the judgment.

TABLE OF CONTENTS

DUE PROCESS

OBTAINING A JUDGMENT IN A MAGISTRATE COURT

CASE PREPARATION

The first order of the day in the collection of any debt, through the assistance of the courts, is obtaining a judgment. Not too many individuals have experience at pursuing a judgment in the courts. Judgments may be obtained in any court. The pursuit of redress is through the judicial procedure permitted under law. This is commonly called *due process*.

To begin the judicial process, a civil complaint must be filed with the court. A complaint alleges the debt or wrong for which redress is requested. The **Georgia Civil Practice Act** requires that the defendant be served with process of summons and complaint **(O.C.G.A. 9-11-13)**.

This service of summons and complaint puts the defendant on formal legal notice, that the plaintiff is seeking redress in the courts, for a debt or other wrong, under the civil code. This is also true of a foreclosure, dispossessory or suit of trover.

The determination of the proper arena and venue is vital to the successful pursuit of a judgment. To determine venue, plaintiff must have the full and proper address of the defendant. Once the address is established, the complaint should be filed in the defendant's county of residence. The process does not begin until the defendant is properly served.

The defendant may decide to acknowledge proper service, but challenge the complaint on proper venue for the filing. Venue is the jurisdiction in which the issue is to be decided. Establishment of venue is set by where the defendant resides or in the case of a corporation, the county where the entity is shown by the Secretary of State as to be incorporated.

The defendant may *traverse* the service of the summons and complaint. A *traverse* is a challenge upon the validity of the service. A *traverse* hearing will be scheduled to decide the issue. The judge will make a determination of whether the service was made properly under the proper legal circumstances such as time and place, etc.

Being properly prepared is critical in achieving the judgment. Being properly prepared will prevent the plaintiff from being intimidated. The plaintiff should attempt to present their case in chronological order as much as is reasonably possible. Logic and patience should control the presentation.

The judgment may be rendered through the decision of a jury, a judge's decision alone in a bench trial, or by the judge based on a default decision. Magistrate Courts in Georgia have jurisdiction over small claims in the amount of $15,000.00 or less.

The plaintiff is not expected to provide overwhelming evidence to prove their case, but the do have prove a preponderance. There are publications available through various bookstores that offer the forms for the filing of civil actions in the Magistrate Courts of Georgia, i.e.; GEORGIA MAGISTRATE COURT GUIDE with forms, by Johnny W. Warren, Attorney at Law, Bay Limited Publications, Inc.

The defendant is required to respond with his answer or other responsive pleadings with thirty (30) days of having been served with the summons and complaint. **(O.C.G.A. 44-14-233) (O.C.G.A. 9-11-12) (GCA 81 A-112).** At or before the time set for the hearing, the defendant may answer in writing or by way of an oral answer.

If the defendant's answer is oral, the substance thereof shall be endorsed by the court on the petition, consisting of any legal or equitable defense or counterclaim. In the case of a foreclosure action or a dispossessory, the defendant has seven days in which to respond.

Whether the plaintiff needs an attorney or not in the Magistrate Courts is really contingent upon their existing knowledge and expertise. It is not mandatory that plaintiffs employ an attorney, but they must be able to exhibit appropriate Courtroom demeanor and follow the accepted rules of evidence.

An enlightened plaintiff, with the proper temperament and perspective, should be able to successfully pursue their case through to collection. The plaintiff should have their facts together and their witnesses subpoenaed for trial. In other words, the plaintiff should be properly and thoroughly prepared.

Once the claim has been filed, the plaintiff should not accept any partial payments while the action is still pending. The plaintiff should accept only payment in full, plus the court costs. Payment should be in cash or some form of certified funds. Any plan for partial payments should be brought before the court.

Although the defendant is technically in default if a response is not made within the thirty (30) days, the default may be reopened as a matter of right, simply by filing an answer within fifteen (15) days immediately after the default judgment and tendering payment of all court costs with the filing of the answer. **(O.C.G.A. 9-11-55(a) (GCA 81A-155)**

If the plaintiff discovers an insufficiency in the filing of the complaint, an amended complaint may be filed **(O.C.G.A. 9-11-15)**. This amended complaint must be filed timely so as to place the defendant on notice as to the new request for redress. This time period for response is not extended by the filing of an amended complaint by the plaintiff.

Day v Norman, 207 GA. App. 37, 427 S.E. 2d 31 (1993)

Rickey E. Tumlin

PRESENTION
OF THE CASE

Presentation of the case or claim begins opening statements that give an overview what it is that you are planning to show the court. Anyone can present a convincing case in court. It only requires confidence in the ability to speak in public and to be able to articulate conclusive, perceptive and relevant questions. Persons of average education, intelligence and vocabulary are more than qualified to present their own case. It just requires common sense and patience.

The plaintiff that represents oneself should be prepared to suffer severe frustrations that might tend to cause one to lose one's temper. Adverse rulings during the proceedings tend to cause people to lose their patience and divert their focus.

Magistrate Court trials are called bench trials and conducted before the magistrate judge only. These are not quite as formal as a trial in a higher court. The level of formality will vary from county to county.

There are no hard and fast rules as to the level of formality desired. This doesn't mean that any improprieties are to be allowed. Strict adherence to the established practices of Courtroom demeanor is expected.

It might serve a plaintiff well to attend a couple of Magistrate Court cases and develop an idea of what may be expected in the presentation of a case. This could very well help to develop some level of confidence and comfort before this type audience and prepare the plaintiff for presenting their own case.

Acquiring some familiarity with the surroundings and becoming comfortable with the subject matter could help to ease later tensions. The taking of notes and seeing the mistakes of others should help tremendously. As with most everything else, the more familiarity you develop, the more comfortable you become with the subject matter. The more comfortable you become, the more you can focus on the issue at hand.

PROVING THE CASE

The trial itself begins with the proving of the claim or complaint. Documentation of the complaint is an absolute must. It is not sufficient to just assert an accusation. A clear and decisive failure of a legal duty on the part of the defendant must be established.

A duty is an obligation or responsibility to perform a specific act or function. This duty can be imposed by statute, contractual agreement, promissory note, or an oath of office, or some other means of obligation. Parents have a duty to provide child support for example.

This duty may be the repayment of a debt owed, debt for services performed, open account, articles purchased or damages incurred, etc. Sometimes this is established very easily with little or no effort on the part of the plaintiff. Other times the skillful evading of questions and creative exaggerations by the defendant or witnesses may cause the plaintiff to be unable to get the testimony that is needed into evidence.

Foremost, the plaintiff must establish; venue, the failure of a legal duty, within the statute of limitations, and a dollar value of damages. There are varying limitation periods for different civil actions. The plaintiff may research these in the local law library.

PRESENTATION OF EVIDENCE

The issue at hand may be proven through the presentation of evidence both physical and testimonial. Testimonial evidence is gained through the sworn testimony of witnesses. These witnesses can be actual eye-witnesses to an event or expert witnesses testifying to matters of fact established through circumstances or examination of physical evidence. Circumstantial evidence alone is not conclusive to gain a decision in favor of the plaintiff.

Once the trial begins is not the time to notify the court that you need to have witnesses come to court. There are proper methods to subpoena your witnesses to appear and be present at court. These procedures are simple and not difficult to understand and follow at all.

The subpoena is issued by the clerk of the court of jurisdiction at the request of the plaintiff or the defendant, for payment of the proper fee. The subpoena can be then presented to the Sheriff for service, also for the proper fee. Any individual of upstanding character, of legal age and having no interest in the outcome of the case may serve the subpoena and not have to pay the Sheriff's fees.

Do not rely on a simple acknowledgment of concession on the part of your witnesses for them to appear. At the last moment, the witness may decide not to appear. If the witnesses are properly subpoenaed, they *have* to appear under penalty of contempt.

A subpoena duces tecum will require the production of relevant documents, records, or other forms of physical evidence in court. If the plaintiff is requesting the production of records in court, it would be advisable to also subpoena the person for the keeping and maintaining of these records. This would be in keeping with the accepted rules of evidence.

Witnesses should be subpoenaed as early as possible to allow for potential delays in service. Witnesses are not always where they can be immediately served with the subpoena and have to be located. Service of the subpoena has to be performed *at least* 24 hours in advance of the appearance to be to be properly enforced. In the case of a subpoena duces tecum, the period is five days.

On occasion, a criminal act can also result in civil liability. This criminal act does not necessarily have to result in a conviction in the criminal court to establish civil liability. This is to say that because a punishment is not imposed for the criminal act, that a civil case can be pursued.

It is entirely possible that a defendant could be exonerated in a criminal court for criminal acts, but still be found liable for damages in a civil court. This has recently been proven in several well publicized celebrity trials in California.

The factors involved in establishing and proving intent in criminal actions are not necessary to find liability for failing to comply with a legal duty or responsibility, or neglect to perform certain acts or duties. It doesn't even necessarily always have to be willful neglect. This could be taken into consideration as a mitigating factor in the rendering of the final judgment.

Hearsay evidence is not admissible into evidence in either a civil or criminal trial. Hearsay is testimony or evidence that is not presented first hand by the person having this knowledge or evidence. This is not to be taken as hearsay evidence being the same as indirect evidence.

The person having the knowledge and making the statement must be available to appear in court as a witness to be cross-examined by the opposing side. Therefore a written statement is not normally admissible. In very limited cases of depositions, both sides are present or represented for proper cross-examination.

Tempers with a short fuse have no place in the Courtroom. A plaintiff should never argue with the witnesses. Proper methods of impeachment should be employed to dispute their testimony. For instance, conflicting statements that may have been made in prior criminal actions may be introduced to impeach a witness.

If there are any doubts about a plaintiff being able to restrain their temper, either in questioning witnesses or in the giving of testimony, it would most likely be best for the plaintiff to employ an attorney to regulate their emotions and properly handle the case for them.

The defendant may be called to the witness stand by the plaintiff for the purposes of cross-examination. **The Fifth Amendment to the United States Constitution** guarantees and protects an individual's right to protection from self incrimination.

This is not a protection in a civil action in the determination of a loss or debt owed. The defendant can be made to testify truthfully under penalty of contempt as to the facts of the issue in question. This also applies to any hearings or depositions as to determine the ownership of any assets that might be subject to levy.

CORPORATE
DEFENDANTS

Substantially, the amount of research invested in the initial stages of debt pursuit can reduce the effort in the latter stages. A judgment that is rendered solely against a corporate defendant may not be pursued through a seizure of non-corporate assets of the corporate officers or other individuals.

Simply because a business has a physical location and is in operation, does not necessarily mean that there will be assets upon which to levy. Nor, does this automatically mean that the business is incorporated.

Collections of judgments against corporate defendants are a little more complex. For a *Fi-Fa* to be enforceable against a corporate defendant, the style of the case must reflect an existing corporate entity. This corporate entity must own and possess tangible assets that would be subject to levy.

Care should be taken not to levy upon any property that readily falls under the exemptions to levy. The contents of the cash register, money box, money drawer, etc., of a defendant business *may* be subject to levy and seizure.

Office furniture, equipment and business machines may be leased or rented. Stock on hand may be on consignment and still belong to the manufacturer or distributor. Tools may belong to the technician employed by the business. Caution should be exercised before seizing items that may not be subject to levy.

You must have the case properly styled to obtain an enforceable judgment. The style of the judgment must be properly mirrored and reflected on the face of the writ. Care should be taken at the outset to properly style the case, giving the complete corporate name of the corporation and its trade name of doing business (**dba**), if there is one. In the case of an individual, the full name of the person and doing business as whatever the business name may be, if not incorporated.

TRADE NAMES

An individual doing business under the name of *'such and such'* is not the same as a corporation. A judgment rendered against a corporation that does not exist, but is in actuality a **dba** business or trade name is not an enforceable judgment. They simply do not have any assets upon which to levy.

Then too, a judgment that is rendered against an individual or individuals is not enforceable against corporate assets. This may determine whether you have an enforceable judgment or not.

These cases are normally styled as: "John Doe dba Blue Mountain Remodeling" for example and the judgment would only being enforceable against John Doe. Blue Mountain Remodeling not being a legal entity, having no legal standing and having no assets, you would pursue and seize the personal property of John Doe.

That the initial filing was styled correctly could become a critical issue if the defendant wants to exercise the opportunity to attempt to conceal assets. The time spent in re-filing or amending the existing complaint could allow sufficient time to transfer ownership or move property in an attempt to conceal or secrete assets to avoid levy.

This transfer of ownership could possibly be set aside or the property eventually located, but would delay the speedy resolution of the judgment. Any and all delays should be considered crucial.

THE JUDGMENT

The decision rendered by the jury or the judge is the judgment. It is then reduced to writing and recorded by the Clerk. The judgment is the plaintiff's basis for obtaining a writ of *fieri facias*. The failure to establish grounds for redress will result in no judgment being rendered.

Judgment and execution are not synonymous terms. This is more than just a matter of semantics. A judgment is the confirmation by the court that the debt is legitimately owed by the defendant. An execution is the tool, vehicle or mechanism whereby the court authorizes the collection of the judgment. Execution is another term for the writ.

Once judgment has been obtained, the plaintiff is entitled to obtain the writ of *Fi-Fa*. The plaintiff is then backed by the full resources of the courts in their efforts to collect. These resources include the levying officer of the Sheriff's office and through the levy officer, the Sheriff, the county attorney, the District Attorney and the judges. To have all the power of the courts behind you is a very powerful collection tool.

The judgment may then be used immediately to secure a writ of *fieri facias*. This writ must then be recoded on the **G.E.D.** in each county where the defendant's property is believed to be located. There will be a fee due the Clerk in each of the counties where the *Fi-FA* is recorded. Once this has been accomplished, a levy may then be executed in the county where the property is discovered to be situated.

WRIT OF FIERI FACIAS

THE WRIT

A writ of *fieri facias* (*Fi-Fa*) is an order which is issued by a judge and directs the levy officer to seize the property of the <u>named</u> defendant. The elements of form for a writ of *fieri facias* are decided and set out by the **Georgia Supreme Court** (form SC-5 revised 1985).

All elements have to be present in the form of the writ for it to be valid and legal. Any deficiency in the form of the writ, not conforming to the dictates of the Georgia Supreme Court, will then result in the *Fi-Fa* not being valid, hence, the writ not being enforceable. In other words, it would not be executable.

For a writ of *fieri facias* to issue, a monetary judgment or judicial award is required. In the case of where judgment is rendered on behalf of the defendant, the writ may properly indicate to collect against the <u>plaintiff</u>. This can be due to the result of a successful defense, a counterclaim or due to other actions of the court.

These issues may be many and widely varied. Judgments may arise from criminal bond forfeiture, lawsuits of various natures, foreclosure, a default in the answering of a garnishment, an award of alimony/child support, etc. A writ of *fieri facias* may be issued from any of the following: judgments, awards, sales taxes, ad valorem taxes, property taxes, income taxes, etc., the foregoing recitation being a very non-inclusive list.

If the '*style*' of the *Fi-Fa,* does not mirror the '*style*' of the judgment, the writ is illegal and is not executable. If the '*style*' of the case on the writ does not reflect the actual name of the corporate entity as it exists with the **Secretary of State**, the writ is illegal and is not executable. So it is paramount that the styling of the case be correct from the outset and throughout the pursuit of the case.

The filing of an appeal automatically places a stay on any attempt at collection or execution of the writ. This is also the case in the filing of a bankruptcy.

ISSUANCE OF THE WRIT

The writ of *fieri facias* can potentially be issued the day the judgment is rendered. This would require the plaintiff making special request for his copy of the judgment and walking it through the process for issuance of a *Fi-Fa*. The *Fi-Fa* should then be taken to the Sheriff's Office.

If the writ of execution is issued before the time period for filing of appeal has expired, execution of the writ is then suspended once the appeal is filed. If the appeal is denied, then the execution is still valid and may be enforced. Normally, the writ is issued by the court granting the judgment.

With some exceptions there is a ten day waiting period from the date of judgment until the actual enforcement of a writ of *fieri facias*. This is intended to permit the defendant the opportunity to satisfy the judgment. This is highly improbable or the debt most likely would have been resolved before reaching this stage.

It is entirely possible that the defendant might take this opportunity to attempt to conceal or secrete their assets in an attempt to avoid a levy. This time period could profitably be spent by the plaintiff in the attempt to locate property upon which to levy. Plaintiff might consult the levy officer for guidance in this pursuit.

The judgment plaintiff must be constantly vigilant in order to not give the defendant the opportunity to out-maneuver their efforts. It would be a shame to have all earlier efforts circumvented by attempts at subterfuge at this point. The plaintiff should keep an eye out for any attempts by the defendant to remove, transfer or conceal assets.

If the writ arises out of a dispossessory action, the writ of *fieri facias* can be used to levy upon the defendant's property during the process of eviction. A plaintiff would have to stay on top of the paperwork and to oversee that everything was completed timely and properly. This constitutes a little difficulty and coordination, but can be done.

THE WRIT
IN GENERAL

Take particular care of the writ of *fieri facias*. Only one *Fi-Fa* will be issued as an original. Copies of a *Fi-Fa* are not enforceable. If a *Fi-Fa* is lost, misplaced, or destroyed, after a very arduous process of documentation, a replacement writ may issue.

This is referred to as an alias *Fi-Fa*. *O.C.G.A 9-13-8* allows for the issuance of an *alias Fi-Fa*. An *alias Fi-Fa* is a duplicate original or replacement *Fi-Fa* and is always subject to the original being produced. This can be compared to the issuing of duplicate titles for automobiles.

The various courts: municipal, magistrate, state, superior and federal all have authority to issue writs of *fieri facias*. Regardless of who issues a writ of *Fi-Fa,* they are all executed in much the same manner.

Judgments from all courts shall be given equal dignity. Dignity, in this instance, meaning priority and consideration. The same laws, rules, conditions, procedures and restrictions shall apply. **O.C.G.A. 19-3-31** requires the Sheriff or his duly authorized levy officer shall execute all writs in the order that they are received.

An execution in favor of the State takes precedence over an execution in favor of an individual, regardless of the judgment date. Individual would also indicate a corporation or business; examples of such would be a criminal bond forfeiture *Fi-Fa* or a tax *Fi-Fa*. An execution in favor of the Federal Government would supersede one in which the State Government is the judgment plaintiff.

The judgment plaintiff may seek assistance and guidance from the Sheriff's Office *Fi-Fa* expert at most any time during normal business hours. It might be advantageous for the plaintiff to stop by the local Sheriff's office to become familiar with the levy officer and maybe pick up any helpful hints or information that they may be able to provide. This may help the plaintiff to become more comfortable in the presence of authority figures and the environment.

SEIZURE OF PROPERTY

The writ must be recorded on the **General Execution Docket (G.E.D.)** of the county where the levy is to be attempted, before the writ may be executed. If the property is mobile and the levy officer follows the property into another county, the property may be returned to the levy officer's county for storage and sale. The levy officer may charge mileage and expenses in this endeavor.

A *Fi-Fa* from another county must first be recorded on the **G.E.D.** of your county before it may be executed, this being where the property allegedly is thought to be located. In the case of mobile property, such as vehicles, boats, trailers, etc., the levy officer may follow this property into another county to prevent the disposal or further concealment of the property.

Once the property has been seized, this property is then published in the legal classifieds of the local *legal organ* and sold at a *Sheriff's Sale* the first Tuesday of the month following publication **(O.C.G.A. 9-13-161a)**. Being set by statute, this is inflexible and must be strictly followed.

The proceeds of this sale are then '*knocked down*' against the judgment and then disbursed by the Sheriff or his lawful deputy, according to law. If the proceeds are sufficient to equal the judgment amount and all costs and fees, the **Fi-Fa** should be marked satisfied and the clerk of court directed to cancel the writ from the General execution Docket, the costs and fees having been first satisfied.

FI-FA TYPES

Overall there are three types of writs of *fieri facias*:

~ *General* - commands the officer to seize all property of the defendant that might be subject to levy.

~ *Specific* - commands the officer to levy on specifically designated property enumerated in the body of the *Fi-Fa*

~ *Combination* - commands the officer to levy on all property belonging to the named defendant and specifically named property.

FOREIGN JUDGMENTS

Judgments from another state must first be carried through the local Superior Court before an attempt to collect can be made. This process is referred to as the *domestication of a foreign judgment.* Foreign relates to having been rendered and issued outside the state of Georgia.

Once the judgment has been domesticated, then a *Fi-Fa* can be issued and recorded on the G.E.D. of the county where the domestication takes place for execution locally. This constitutes confirmation or an affirmation of the judgment and the authorization for local enforcement.

The domestication process need not be pursued but once. If the defendant should move to another county within the state, plaintiff need only take the *Fi-Fa* arising from the domesticated judgment, to the county of residence and have it recorded on the **G.E.D.** there.

Rickey E. Tumlin

POST JUDGMENT INTEREST

Effective July 1, 2003 **O.C.G.A. 7-4-10** sets the legal rate of interest at the prevailing prime rate plus 3 per cent in effect at the time of judgment. A free calculator for the calculation of interest may be downloaded from the website:

http://www.pine-grove.com

and by downloading: 'Loan Calculator*Plus, Version 2.1'

Judgments rendered from July 1, 1986 till July 1, 2003 are entitled to accrue interest at the rate of twelve per cent. These *Fi-Fa's* that have been rerecorded and current are still enforceable. The twelve per cent rate still applies.

Under the old method of calculation, the author had attempted to be consistent by always calculating the interest by the month. Now that it is becoming more intricate and involved, mistakes can more easily be made.

Some attorneys insist on dividing the annual interest by three hundred and sixty-five days, and then multiply by the number of days from the judgment date. It is probably best then to leave the calculation of interest to the plaintiff or their attorney. If there should be any disputes, the defendant should make timely appeal to the court.

If the levy officer is put on the spot to calculate the interest, it is best to itemize the steps and permanently document the calculations. This should also be placed in the Clerk's permanent file. Copies of all receipts rendered should be maintained permanently.

DUTIES OF
THE SHERIFF

SHERIFF'S DUTIES
IN GENERAL

The Sheriff of the county is a Constitutional Officer, an officer of the court and the highest law enforcement official in the county. The duties of the Sheriff are extensive and widely varied. All the Constitutional duties of the Sheriff are viewed as equally important under the law. The primary duties of the Sheriff consist of:

1 ~ the service and execution of warrants

2 ~ duties as bailiff to the various courts

3 ~ service of summonses ad subpoenas under **O.C.G.A. 44-14-232**

4 ~ service of other civil process and precepts as prescribed by law

5 ~ to keep and maintain the common jail of the county

6 ~ custodian of the Courthouse of the county

These are only a very small portion of the duties of the Sheriff, but are essentially the primary duties and by far consume the majority of his attention. Since this publication concerns the collection of judgments, the author will not diverge in to the other responsibilities of the Sheriff or his office at this time.

FAILURE TO ACT

A failure to act on the part of the Sheriff or his lawful deputy could lead to an accusation of **malfeasance**, **misfeasance** or **nonfeasance** and if determined to be valid, possibly could result in citation for contempt, judgment for damages, removal from office or other lawful sanctions imposed.

The principle of vicarious liability is the vehicle that makes the Sheriff liable for the actions of his duly appointed deputies. Being aware of this, you can rest assured that the levy officer is going to take great pains to be sure that everything is done correctly. This is another reason for emphasis on the documentation of activity.

RECORD KEEPING

SHERIFF'S RECORDS

O.C.G.A. 15-16-10a(4) requires the Sheriff to maintain bound copies of the newspaper selected as the legal organ in the same manner as required by law for the Clerk of the Superior Court. This can be used as a permanent research reference of prior sales.

The Sheriff may enter into a contractual agreement with the Clerk of the Superior Court or the Judge of Probate to maintain a joint permanent record of the legal organ. Such contractual arrangement should be reduced to writing and recorded in the records of the Clerk of Superior Court. Times being what they are, strict adherence to following the statutes is emphasized.

O.C.G.A. 15-16-10a(5) requires the Sheriff to keep and maintain an execution docket wherein he must enter a full description of all executions delivered to him and the dates of their delivery, together with his actions thereon, and to have the same ready for use in any court of his county.

This execution docket encompasses all writs of execution, including but not limited to writs of possession, *Fi-Fa's*, transport orders or any order issued by a judge, normally bearing a case or docket number and directs the Sheriff or his lawful deputies to perform a particular act or duty.

O.C.G.A. 15-16-10a(6) requires the Sheriff to keep and maintain a book in which shall be entered a record of all sales made by process of court or by agreement of the parties under the sanction of the court, describing accurately the property and the process under which sold, the date of the levy and sale, the purchaser and price.

This record book should be a permanently bound volume, that when completed should be filed with the Clerk of Superior Court for permanent record. This documentation may be done on the computer and maintained as other such official computer records are kept for retrieval.

O.C.G.A. 15-16-11 requires that all docket books which the Sheriff is required to keep, after becoming full must be deposited in the office of the **Clerk of Superior Court**, to be kept as are other books of record, provided, however that record which the Sheriff is required to keep and which are computerized shall be maintained and stored for computer retrieval in the office of the Sheriff.

The establishment of a detailed record-keeping system by the Sheriff is of the utmost importance, in addition to being required by statute. An automated date-stamp machine is a terrific method of documentation of receipt and is highly recommended by the author. Entry of all information in the Sheriff's docket book is essential.

An accurate and detailed method of record keeping can eliminate a majority of the potential problems and the minimizing of possible liability that could arise down the road. Most documentation can be recorded or placed in the original case file of the Clerk of Court. The consequences of sloppy or inadequate record keeping have the potential of being a liability disaster for everyone involved.

EXECUTING A LEVY

PRE-LEVY
PREPARATION

A levy is the seizure of property belonging to the <u>named</u> defendant in the style of the *Fi-Fa*, pursuant to the order. It is the plaintiff's responsibility to uncover and locate any assets belonging to the defendant.

The property must belong legally and totally to the defendant in *Fi-Fa* A pre-levy interview with the plaintiff noting any partial payment s that have been made towards satisfying the judgment should be conducted.

The plaintiff should be led through an outline or scenario of the levy process that is to occur and what is to be expected of them. The plaintiff should be instructed that every detail need to be brought forth at this time.

The levy officer should instruct the plaintiff that no altercation is to occur, no matter the provocation. The plaintiff should be advised that this is not a method to exact revenge or to satisfy a personal vendetta.

A determination of ownership and any prior outstanding liens should be established before attempting to execute a levy, if at all possible. This responsibility lies with the plaintiff. The property must be unencumbered, free and clear.

U.C.C. filings are most commonly made by lenders when professionals, such as doctors, attorneys, etc., place their office equipment, furnishings, medical equipment, law library, and so forth up as collateral. These filings extend to many other facets of the business community.

There can be no mortgages, liens, deed to secure debt or **U.C.C.** filings against the property upon which you are about to levy. **U.C.C.** filings may be checked via the internet at:

http://www.gsccca.org/search/UCC_Search/default.asp

Due to the principle of vicarious liability, the levying officer's supervisor should be as meticulous as the levy officer himself. Responsibility for everything having been done correctly ultimately lies with the Sheriff. It stands to reason that the Sheriff will have highly competent individuals in these positions.

THE LEVY

19-13-10 OFFICIAL CODE OF GEORGIA ANNOTATED (O.C.G.A.) requires the Sheriff or his lawful deputy, to make levys pursuant to a writ of *fieri facias (Fi-Fa)* or other writ of attachment on the property, either real or personal or both, of the defendant in *Fi-Fa* A levy is a seizure of property to pursuant to a lawful order from a court. A judge may issue an order constituting a writ of execution, directing the levy officer to levy and seize specific property and sell at judicial sale as in a writ of *Fi-Fa*

The concept of a levy and seizure under *Fi-Fa* is a very powerful tool in the collection of judgments. This is due to the inherent power to deprive persons of their lawfully obtained property. The principle, when properly pursued and executed, can be exceptionally effective. The pursuit of garnishment can be equally effective but not as intimidating.

A 'judgment' is the debt of record, the *Fi-Fa* is the mechanism used to enforce the judgment. If the judgment has been paid, the process is functus officio. (*This term is applied to something which once had life and power,, but which now has no virtue whatsoever; as, for example, a warrant of attorney on which a judgment has been entered is functus officio, and a second judgment cannot be entered by virtue of its authority.*) The execution of a writ that is no longer valid is an unlawful levy. An unlawful levy is not synonymous with an illegal levy or an improper levy, though there is some liability with each.

A levy is a method in law by which plaintiffs may recover judgments rendered and handed down by the courts. A levy is not always the quickest method of collection, but by far is the more intimidating of the alternatives. The potential loss of acquired personal property is daunting, to say the very least. To unlawfully remove a person's property is to deny them their Constitutional rights. Strict adherence to the proper steps under due process is the only protection from liability.

A levy carries an extremely high level of potential liability, possibly equaled only by that of excessive use of force. The duty and responsibility on behalf of the levy officer to follow all steps and procedures is inherently intimidating.

Trial and error is definitely not the preferred method to pursue in the execution of a levy. The *Fi-Fa* expert in your Sheriff's office is your most readily accessible source of information. The levy officer is not permitted to give legal advice, but can help you explore and ascertain the available methods of collection.

Judgment plaintiffs who regularly, as part of their course of business, engage in the collection of judgments would do well to familiarize themselves with their local *Fi-Fa* expert in the Sheriff's office and become acquainted with the procedures involved. Familiarity with the process and procedures can help to expedite the levy attempt at a time when speed could be essential.

Some defendants can be very persuasive. They can really relate some awful tales of woe. The levy officer should refrain from openly appearing sympathetic to either side. To do so only evokes feelings of resentment from the other side. The levy officer is not present to take sides, but to execute an order of the court.

LOCATION AND IDENTIFICATION OF DEFENDANT PROPERTY

It is the responsibility of the plaintiff to ascertain and locate property of the judgment defendant that would sufficient to satisfy the judgment. There are various methods that may be employed using numerous resources. It is hoped that this publication alerts the plaintiff to resources that are available.

The most common of which is the acquiring of automobile tags on vehicles possessed by the defendant. In the case where the plaintiff has located a vehicle upon which he might designate levy, law enforcement assistance can be requested in establishing ownership.

The plaintiff may wish to go to the Clerk of Court's deed room to seek out ownership of real estate. After exhausting all other avenues of collection, the plaintiff may levy on the defendant's real estate.

INTERROGATORIES

Plaintiffs should never underestimate the value of interrogatories. Interrogatories are a key element of the discovery process. Interrogatories can help to expedite the identification of assets belonging to the defendant in *Fi-Fa* the timely filing of a request for interrogatories can greatly reduce the amount of time, effort and expense expended in the collection of their judgment.

The Magistrate Court discovery process is applicable to judgments rendered from any court. When filed timely, interrogatories can be an invaluable aid in the pursuit of collection of the judgment and at minimal cost. When used and enforced properly, interrogatories can be highly instrumental in the detection and location of a defendant's assets. Again, these costs incurred are minimal and ultimately recoverable from the judgment defendant. These filing fees are actual court costs.

Post-judgment interrogatories are a set of questions that the judgment plaintiff may have served on the defendant, requiring the revelation of any and all assets that might be subject to levy or garnishment. Failure of the defendant to completely, truthfully and responsibly answer to the interrogatories may be punishable by citation for contempt.

Pre-judgment interrogatories may be issued if there is substantial risk that the assets may be disposed of or removed from the jurisdiction of the court. Delays in the filing of interrogatories could result in greater fees for issuance.

PROPERTY
SUBJECT TO LEVY

O.C.G.A. 9-13-50 allows for the defendant in *Fi-Fa* to be permitted the option to designate what property shall be levied upon, subject to the levying officer's opinion that said property is sufficient to satisfy the judgment and costs. The working phrase here is 'the levying officer's opinion'.

The defendant is seldom ever willing to participate in this stage of the levy. Should the defendant insist on designating property that is immediately apparent as to not be sufficient to satisfy the judgment, it should be taken as nonparticipation by the defendant.

Failure to designate property upon which to levy, for whatever reason, does not stay execution of the writ.

L.R. Sams v. Hardy, 218 Ga. 147, 126 S.E.2d 661 (1962)

When property designated by the defendant in *Fi-Fa* is in the possession of someone not a party to the judgment from which the judgment is issued, the Sheriff or other levying officer shall not levy thereupon, but should seize such property to be found in the actual possession of defendant. There are some exceptions to this rule.

An exception to this applicability is whereby the plaintiff/claimant points out the property of the defendant upon which to be levyed and sold.

City of Leesburg v. Forrester, 59 Ga. App. 503, 1 S.E.2d 584 (1939)

This being the case, the plaintiff may then designate the property whereupon which to levy.

Benson & Coleman v. Dyer, 69 Ga. 190 (1982)

The levy officer is not expected to be an expert in the valuation of property that may be subject to seizure by levy.

Planters Bank v. Georgia Loan & Trust Co., 160 Ga. 107 (1,b) (127 S.E. 413) and citations

LEVY PRACTICES

Established practices in the method of levy have developed over many decades and have thus been confirmed via case law. The documentation of established practices and traditional procedures has helped to lay the groundwork for a majority of the judicial decisions. The method or procedure by which a levy or seizure is made is pretty much set by statute and supplemented by case law, but is still somewhat generic in nature.

Some statutes may appear to be in conflict and at times may seem to appear ambiguous. If this ever appears to be the case, the levy officer should not hesitate to consult with the county attorney. In most cases, it only requires a little clarification of the *'legalese'*.

The levy officer should never attempt to execute a copy of a writ of *Fi-Fa.* The original writ should *always be in hand* when making an attempt at collection or levy. A copy of the document has no legal standing and is *never* executable. A copy of a writ or even a certified copy of the writ of *fieri facias* is not the same as an ***alias Fi-Fa***

The amount of case law concerning levys is limited and much is governed by rulings recorded in the old English common law. This has long been an established practice of the courts of our land.

This leaves much to interpretation by the individual courts and judges. Any conflict between established practices and procedures and the issuing judge should be referred to the county attorney for reconciliation.

The levy officer should never take anything for granted. Just because a plaintiff or his attorney relates some particular information does not necessarily meant that it is reliable or accurate. This is not to imply that the plaintiff or his attorney would intentionally do anything improper, but no one is infallible. The direction provided by the county attorney or your judge should be your guide.

A failure to accurately determine a particular fact uttered by anyone could result in liability for the levy officer, his supervisors and ultimately the Sheriff. It is rare that incidents of these types occur. On the rare occasion that they do happen, it is usually out of unintentional ignorance of the law. This may not be sufficient protection in the case of a defendant filing a grievance action.

It has been the author's experience that many, many attorneys have little or no experience with *Fi-Fa's* and levys. Research and documentation should become by-words for the levy officer. Make an attempt to confirm the lack of outstanding liens yourself. Check to make sure that any lien shown is still current and outstanding.

Be tactful and diplomatic in your interaction, but scrutinize everything carefully. Double check everything and document your efforts. The levy officer should be careful to refrain from ambiguous actions or unclear communication at all times. The levy officer should also be insistent and clear on the matter of not giving legal advice to anyone.

Record all information obtained from each and every source. Again, the emphasis is on documentation. This very well may make the difference in a successful levy and sale or lawsuit.

AUTHORITY
FOR THE LEVY

The levy officer should always bear in mind that actions taken are under the authority of and at the direction of the court. The plaintiff is the direct beneficiary of these actions, but the property seized is in reality the possession of the court issuing the judgment, although it is indirectly through the levy officer. All the while the levy officer is acting as an agent for the defendant. That being the case, any appeals, motions or requests for stays must be filed with and decisions issued by that court. Note where on the writ it says it is returnable to the issuing court.

For a levy to be valid, the property must be seized in a manner sufficient to demonstrate actual or constructive custody/possession by the court. Sufficient steps must be taken so as to place the defendant on notice that the property has been seized. Once seized, entry of the seizure should be made upon the writ.

The levy officer must commit an act that would otherwise be considered an act of trespass, were it not for the protection of the writ. When all steps are properly executed, the levy officer is afforded the protection of the court from civil liability.

Property seized by an officer at the request of a judgment-plaintiff is technically in actuality being held on behalf of and in the possession of the court. A levy on real estate (real property) does not require actual physical seizure, but must meet the definition of a constructive seizure. The levy on real estate is to be entered on the **G.E.D.** and notice given to the defendant/tenant in possession to be a valid levy.

Once the goods or property are successfully seized and properly stored, this property must then be published in the legal classifieds of the local *legal organ* and sold at a Sheriff's Sale the first Tuesday in the month immediately following publication of the fourth insertion. (**O.C.G.A. 9-13-161a**) The proceeds of this sale are then '*knocked* *down*' against the judgment and then disbursed by the Sheriff as prescribed by law. (**O.C.G.A. 9-13-60**)

This '*knockdown*' may or may not satisfy the judgment. If sufficient to satisfy the judgment, the satisfaction portion of the writ should be completed and cleared from the **Superior Court Clerk's General Execution Docket**. If insufficient to satisfy the judgment, this '*knockdown*' should be entered and additional levys may be made or other methods pursued to completely satisfy the judgment. These other methods may include garnishment proceedings.

DOCUMENTING
THE SEIZURE

Once the seizure has been effected, it must be entered on the *Fi-Fa* before the levy is complete. This is described as making a return of levy. **O.C.G.A. 15-13-14** requires that if any Sheriff or *other officer* fails to make a proper return of all writs, executions, and other processes placed into his hands or fails to pay over all moneys received on such executions, upon his being required to do so by the court, he shall be <u>liable for contempt and may be fined, imprisoned, or removed from office in the manner prescribed by the Constitution and laws of the state of Georgia</u>.

O.C.G.A. 18-3-31 requires that in all cases it shall be the duty of the officer levying attachments to levy them in the order in which they come into his hands and it shall be his duty to enter upon the same the year, month, day and hour on which he made the levy. These efforts shall be timely and according to applicable law. These efforts at documentation may then be placed in the Clerk of Courts file as a part of the permanent record.

You should document all efforts and attempts to reasonably identify the value and ownership of the property levyed. This will help to avert attempts to allege excessive over levy.

Planters Bank v. Georgia Loan & Trust Co., 160 Ga. 107 (1,b) (127 S.E. 413) and citations

CONTROL OF THE WRIT OF FIERI FACIAS

The plaintiff in *Fi-Fa* or his attorney has total and absolute control over the *Fi-Fa*. Only the plaintiff or his attorney may request that the clerk of the court issue a *Fi-Fa*. The plaintiff or his attorney may also cancel or suspend any efforts at levy or collection. This is another good reason for the levy officer to get levy fees and all other costs up front, also a good reason to document your efforts and circumstances.

The plaintiff, his attorney or his lawful agent can demand possession of the *Fi-Fa* and is required to only return it the day of the judicial sale. It is not advisable to go ahead and conduct the Sheriff's Sale without the possession of the original *Fi-Fa*. The original writ should be in the sale officer's actual possession during the Sheriff's Sale.

In the case of multiple levys, it may require some juggling to get the *Fi-Fa* from one jurisdiction to the other on the day of the sale, so as to be able to conduct multiple judicial sales. All '*knockdowns*' should be entered on the writ before it is released to be taken to another jurisdiction. This is logistically possible with the legal hours of sale ranging over the six hour period from 10:00 am to 4:00pm on the sale day.

Suggestion to levy officer: Place copies of all written correspondence related to the writ and it execution in the Clerk's file. Hence, this documentation may be accessed by anyone wishing to review actions taken concerning the collection without fear of loss of the documents. Any pertinent notes or observations made by the officer should also be placed in the file.

LEVYING ON PROPERTY UNDER LIEN

Under most circumstances, property subject to a prior outstanding lien is not subject to levy. In cases where the property's value greatly exceeds the outstanding lien may be subject to levy if:

a.) The lien-holder agrees to allow the plaintiff in *Fi-Fa* to pay off the lien. Said payoff amount is recoverable from the proceeds of the sale before any 'knockdown' takes place.

b.) The lien-holder agrees to waive his lien, subject to being paid first from the sale proceeds before any 'knockdown' occurs.

It is the plaintiff's duty to ascertain any property that might be subject to levy. There are instances whereby the levy officer is required to assist in the determination of ownership, but ostensibly, it falls on the plaintiff to do the research and location of the property. The plaintiff may seek guidance in his efforts from the Sheriff's Office levy expert.

If a defendant willfully, actively and/or forcefully, attempts to interdict, obstruct or otherwise prevent the execution of lawful levy, they *may* possibly be charged with the criminal offense of *obstruction of an officer*. Depending upon the circumstances and the degree of force used, this may possibly be charged as a felony. Every effort should be made to execute the writ without having to resort to this alternative.

There are seldom any serious challenges to an officer's levy and seizure. This is much in part due to the inexperience of most attorneys in dealing with *Fi-Fa's* and levys. It has been pretty much a given that if the levy officer is acting with reasonable prudence and in good faith, he will not be held liable for his actions.

MULTIPLE LEVYS

Multiple levys, pursuant to the same *Fi-Fa* on the same or subsequent days are permissible, as long as there is not an over-levy. Sheriff's Sales as a rule, usually net only a minor fraction of the actual value of the property sold. In the event that the only property subject to levy greatly exceeds the judgment, there is no other alternative but to seize that property. This decidedly should be documented.

Additional levys may be conducted in other counties on the same writ at the same time that a Sheriff's Sale could be pending. The plaintiff may take the *Fi-Fa* to another jurisdiction for an additional levy. Thus it is imperative that the levy return be entered so as to alert other officers of the possibility that an over levy could potentially occur.

The judgment plaintiff or his attorney or agent may carry the writ from one agency to another, performing whatever additional levy's may be necessary to satisfy the judgment. The *Fi-Fa* should be timely returned for the Sheriff's Sale.

It is the judgment-plaintiff's responsibility to locate/determine what personal property of the defendant, if any, that may be subject to levy. Diligent pursuit of defendant property can be time consuming and frustrating. The reward is the location of assets sufficient to satisfy the judgment.

This property should be free and clear from any prior outstanding liens, mortgages or other encumbrances. The levying officer should be cautioned against just taking someone's word that there are no outstanding liens on the subject property. Independent research on the part of the levy officer should be exercised to determine or confirm that the property is unencumbered. Every effort should be made that any existing liens not be overlooked.

If the plaintiff in *Fi-Fa* elects to pay off the debt so that the defendant in *Fi-Fa* has full and legal title to the property, then the plaintiff can levy on the property. This is subject to the party holding the debt or lien consents to allowing the plaintiff to pay off the debt. The levy officer may need to obtain clarification from your county attorney before the exercising of this option.

OVER LEVY

Caution should be exercised not to over-levy or to execute an excessive levy. The levy Officer should take care to reasonably assess the value of the property. It is unlawful to excessively over levy. That is when the value of the property seized is of conspicuous value in excess of the judgment amount.

It is incumbent upon the levying officer to ultimately decide if it appears that the property excessively exceeds the judgment. This responsibility and liability ultimately extends to the Sheriff.

Seizing property where the value greatly exceeds the judgment is difficult to avoid when the property seized is the only property available. In this case there would be no alternative but to seize the available property.

Sometimes it is difficult to judge the value of certain types of property, antiques for an example. You may wish to seek an outside opinion from someone that has experience in the particular field of expertise. If this is done, the levy officer should document the opinion. If expense is to be incurred for the opinion, it should be borne by the plaintiff.

The officer levying a *Fi-Fa* can exercise reasonable discretion as to the sufficiency of the property to satisfy the execution and should be allowed a reasonable margin between the value of the property levied upon and the amount of the *Fi-Fa*:

Planters Bank v. Georgia Loan & Trust Co., 160 Ga. 107 (1,b) (127 S.E.413) and citations

The levy officer should always exercise caution in estimating the value of property so as not to over-levy. On the rare occasion that this should occur, it is usually out of unintentional ignorance and inexperience on the part of the levying officer as to the market value of the property. This is also influenced by the market demand for the particular property. Seized property almost never brings the amount estimated by the levy officer. The levy officer is not expected to be an expert in the valuation of any property.

WRONGFUL LEVY

If you levy upon property in the possession of and belonging to some person who is not the defendant in *Fi-Fa*, without probable cause, you are a trespasser even if directed to do so by plaintiff's attorney. The levy officer is expected to exercise prudence in his actions. **(O.C.G.A. 51-10-1)**

If plaintiff's attorney directs that the seizure be made without probable cause, he is a joint trespasser in conjunction with his client. **O.C.G.A. 9-3-90** through **O.C.G.A. 9-13-106** covers claims made by third parties to the property seized. Remember, everything is judged and decided on the actions of a *prudent* individual.

Exercise caution in the seizure of property where ownership is claimed by a third party. The levy officer is expressly forbidden by law from an act of over-levy, wrongful levy, illegal seizure and any other acts protected by the **Fourth and fourteenth Amendments to the United States Constitution** and the applicable sections of the **Constitution of the state of Georgia**. As long as the levy officer is recognized as exercising due and careful diligence, it is unlikely that they would suffer any liability.

The levy officer should always bear in mind that he is acting as an agent of the Sheriff, on behalf of the court and at court's direction, to benefit the plaintiff while protecting the rights of the defendant. Doing so will assure that the defendant's rights under the **Fourth and Fourteenth Amendments to the U.S. Constitution** are protected.

In order to successfully levy, the levying officer must commit some act for which he could otherwise be prosecuted for trespass if it were not for the protection afforded by the court under the writ. If the officer executes a wrongful levy, he may be sued in civil court. **O.C.G.A. 51-10-1** covers wrongful levy and the unauthorized seizure of personal property. Any ambiguity on the part of the levy officer's actions could leave the door open to allege a possible wrongful levy.

A prudent officer, observing due caution and exercising all available resources, will avoid most pitfalls of this nature. Following the proper steps, it is rare that any of these types of incidents will occur. The levy officer has to be ever diligent, ever watchful and ever cautious in the execution of his duties. This is why proper documentation is so very critical.

TYPES OF SEIZURE

This seizure can be actual or constructive. Physical seizure is where the property levied upon is taken from the site and placed in storage. Constructive seizure is where the property may have to be left where it sits due to logistics or other factors as in the case of real estate, but sufficient action has been taken to put the defendant on notice that the property has been seized under levy. A notice of levy and sale should then be attached to the property in a manner such that all might see.

The plaintiff has great latitude in directing what might be seized. The contents of an individual's pockets, purse and even the jewelry on their person may be subject to seizure. Property in the immediate physical or constructive possession of the defendant in *Fi-Fa* may be subject to levy. If the levy attempt is upon a vehicle don't overlook the contents, such as in dash pockets, door pockets, glove box, or the trunk. Never overlook any viable possibility.

Note: Any property that may have been pledged as collateral on the original debt, from which the judgment resulted, though it may be subject to levy, does not necessarily have to be the objective of the levy. This possibly could be the case if you have a special *Fi-Fa* normally, under most circumstances, it can be any property owned by the defendant.

The judgment plaintiff should be instructed to always follow the lead of the levying officer. The plaintiff should take care to listen and to absorb all that the defendant has to say regarding ownership of any questionable property or their financial situation. Some defendants will recant earlier comments with conflicting statements or clues to property, subject to possible levy, that were otherwise undisclosed.

At no time should the plaintiff be permitted to provoke the defendant into a physical encounter. This is not an opportunity for anyone to seek revenge. The levy officer must attempt to maintain the proper demeanor and decorum for the activity at all times. To allow anything else is to invite an incident resulting in liability.

LEVY UPON AUTOMOBILES

When levying upon an automobile, be sure to check for any outstanding liens. Judgment holders may carry their judgment *Fi-Fa* to the Tax Commissioner of the county where the defendant resides (or where suspected vehicles might be registered) and upon presentation of the writ, determine if any automobiles are registered in the name of the defendant.

The author has found that some Tax Commissioners favor making a photo-copy of the writ for placement in their files. This information may also be obtained from the **Georgia Division of Motor Vehicle Services** via written request and accompanied by a certified copy of the *Fi-Fa.*

Further information and forms may be obtained at their website:

http://www.dmvs.ga.gov/forms//motor.asp

In the case where the plaintiff has located a vehicle upon which he might designate levy, law enforcement assistance can be requested.

In this case the plaintiff brings a tag number to the law enforcement agency to determine legal ownership. It does not have to necessarily be a Sheriff's Office to make this request.

O.C.G.A. 40-2-130c authorizes any law enforcement officer in Georgia to assist the plaintiff *only* to determine if the vehicle is owned by the defendant in *Fi-Fa* and if there are any outstanding liens. This **does not** permit the disclosure of *any* information if the vehicle is found to belong to someone other than the defendant in *Fi-Fa.*

If a lien is determined, check with the lien-holder of record to ascertain if the lien is still valid. If the lien has been paid, the vehicle may be subject to levy. In some cases the lien has been paid off for quite some time, but the owner has neglected to have the lien removed from the title of ownership, possibly even intentionally. This is usually in an effort to discourage judgment plaintiffs from possible levy attempts.

If a defendant purports to have placed the vehicle title up for collateral, as at a loan company, finance company, bank, or a title-pawn establishment, check it out. The lien must be recorded with the **Department of Revenue - Motor Vehicle Services Division** for the lien to be valid. This is easily discernible through the local county Tax Commissioner's office or through the **Georgia Department of Motor Vehicle Services** computer.

Since current Georgia law requires that license plates remain with the vehicle owner, it would be advisable to remove the plate and leave it with the registered owner/defendant at the time of levy and seizure. This would prevent any later accusations of wrongful seizure of the license plate.

The author has encountered multiple instances of where these title pawn businesses have foreclosed on a delinquent loan, sold the automobile, left the license plate on the vehicle and an insurance card in the dash pocket. Both the license plate and the insurance card are still legally the property of the defendant.

If the vehicle is in a repair shop and is being held subject to payment for the repair, the repairman has a vested first lien by virtue of simple possession of the automobile. This might not be true if there has been no repair yet and no bill due. Check with your local county attorney.

The payment of the cost of the repair by the plaintiff versus the value of the vehicle, for the purposes of a possible levy, might be worthy of consideration. This would be subject to the repair facility agreeing to permit the seizure.

The judgment creditor may elect to negotiate with the repairman or other lien holder for the authorization to levy on the automobile. The negotiation can be for the plaintiff to make actual payment of the outstanding lien or debt, or through the promise of payment via the proceeds of the Sheriff's Sale.

It would be advisable for the results of these negotiations to be documented in a written agreement signed by both parties. It would not necessarily be inappropriate for the officer to affix his signature to the agreement as a witness. This should hinge on individual departmental policy. This agreement could then be placed in the Clerk's permanent file.

The levy officer should refrain from becoming involved in these negotiations. The levy officer should not place the integrity of the Sheriff's Office at risk at any time. This places clear title in the name of the defendant for the purposes of levy. The repairman's bill is subject to payment before any *'knockdown'*. The responsibility lies with the Sheriff's Office in the disbursing of the proceeds.

LEVYING ON
PERSONAL PROPERTY
(Any Property Other Than Real Estate)

This is any tangible property established as belonging to the defendant in *Fi-FA*. This property can be automobiles, boats/boat trailers, utility trailers, tools, furniture, appliances, equipment, the contents of their pockets, etc. Virtually any property that is not real estate is personal property. An exception might be property that is considered assets of a corporation. It is still personal property, but belongs to a corporation.

LEVYING ON
REAL ESTATE
(Real Property)

Real estate (land) may not be levied upon until all other efforts at collection have been exhausted, with the exception of a property-tax *Fi-Fa*. In this case you should levy on nothing but the land that is subject to the property-taxation. Tax *Fi-Fa's* always follow the land.

In the event that real estate is the only property upon which to levy, it would be a very good idea to document this fact. Documentation is definitely recommended and always a good practice. Again, this documentation should be placed in the Clerk's permanent file.

Notice of intent to levy is not necessary to be given in advance. However, notice must be given within five days of the execution of the levy by giving notice to the defendant/tenant in possession of the land; give notice to the defendant separately if residing within the county, or by first class mail to the defendant residing outside the county within the five day constraint. *(The author feels that it would be a good practice to go ahead and send out a written notice of levy and sale by first class or even certified mail to the defendant in any event.)*

O.C.G.A. 18-3-31 indicates that in all cases it shall be the duty of the officer who is levying attachments to levy the executions in order in which they come into his hands, and it shall be his duty to enter upon the same the day, month, year and hour on which he made the levy.

Where the levy is upon land, the attachment must be entered on the execution or attachment docket **(G.E.D.)** by the clerk of the Superior Court in order to be good against third persons acting in good faith and without actual notice. Proper legal notice should be given to the defendant and to the tenant in possession if not occupied by the defendant.

The levy officer should take special care to not overlook the level of liability involved in the execution of a levy. The levy officer is under an extensive duty to not infringe upon the rights of the defendant while the plaintiff's rights are being exercised. The levy officer must remain unbiased throughout the process and give no appearance of judicial prejudice.

FUNDAMENTALS
OF LEVY

Fundamentally, the levy process begins with the monetary demand for payment. *Whatever* the reason for failure to pay, it is considered to be nonpayment. In the event of nonpayment, the defendant is notified that they have the opportunity to designate that of their property which they wish to be levied upon, ***sufficient*** to satisfy the judgment. Note that this right is conditional upon the property being sufficient to satisfy the judgment.

This is the point that will most likely provoke a confrontational response, if it is going to occur. Most times the defendant declares that they have nothing upon which to levy. Some go so far as to advise you, and not too politely, that you are not going to take anything of theirs. There are some occasions where this is done to provoke a violent response out of the plaintiff or levy officer in an attempt to achieve some standing for a civil suit. It would be an understatement to say that the levy officer must use patience and restraint in dealing with both plaintiffs and defendants.

Upon a failure by the defendant to designate property upon which to levy, for whatever reason, the levying officer then asks the plaintiff which property of the defendant they wish to designate to levy upon, sufficient to satisfy the judgment. This has most times already been discussed in advance, in the event that the levy process might proceed beyond this point. This allows for a smooth and orderly progression of events. Indecision is sometimes misinterpreted by the defendant as a lack of legal or official standing.

The levy officer should be very clear in this activity and vocalize these steps to afford the defendant no opportunity for misunderstanding. This is to officially put the defendant on notice that his property is being seized by the courts, subject to a lawful order. This keeps the defendant apprised of what is taking place and protects the levy officer.

The levy officer should make it clear to the plaintiff that the levy is being made by the courts and the property is in the court's possession, even though the plaintiff is directing the levy to be executed and is assuming responsibility and liability for the storage of the seized property. The levy officer must make it clear to the defendant that the property is being seized by the court.

LEVY STEPS

It would be good practice to walk the plaintiff through the steps of a model levy and seizure. This will help the plaintiff to become a little more comfortable with the process and help them be aware of what might be expected of them. A very real oversimplification of the steps in performing the execution of levy may be broken down as follows:

1. ~ monetary demand for payment of judgment

2. ~ requesting that the <u>defendant</u> designate what property they wish to be levied upon

3. ~ requesting of the <u>plaintiff</u> which of defendant's property that they wish to be levied upon

4. ~ seizure of the property

5. ~ storage arrangements for the property at a secure location, pending sale

6. ~ placing of the legal advertisement for the sale

7. ~ conducting of the Sheriff's sale

8. ~ the knockdown of the proceeds of the sale

9. ~ satisfaction of the judgment and subsequent cancellation on the **G.E.D.**

These steps are all accentuated with relevant explanations as needed given to the defendant. Explanations help to eliminate most misconceptions and misunderstandings.

STORAGE AND PRESERVATION OF THE PROPERTY

It is ultimately the plaintiff's responsibility to make all arrangements and to be responsible for the expense of towing, storage, etc., of all levied property. These costs are recoverable from the proceeds of the sheriff's sale before any '*knockdown*' occurs. '*Knockdown*' is the term applied to the process to dispose of property to a bidder at an auction sale; hence the disposal of the property at a judicial or Sheriff's sale "knocks down" the judgment by the amount netted or realized from the proceeds of the sale.

A little bit of comparison shopping amongst the storage facilities can save several dollars that can then be effectively applied to the judgment principal. Some storage lot owners, when made aware of the circumstances of it being a levy, will negotiate for a lesser rate. Careful scheduling of the levy, relative to the publication and sale dates, can minimize the storage fees even further.

Property seized under levy should be stored at a secure location inside the county where the seizure was performed or if circumstances dictate differently, the county where the sale is to take place, preferably a bonded and insured storage facility. Plaintiff may elect to store the property levied upon themselves, but should bear in mind that they most likely will be held liable by the court in case of theft, loss, or damage.

Plaintiff should note that if the seized property fails to produce sufficient proceeds at the Sheriff's Sale to offset the costs incurred, plaintiff is liable for the difference. All reasonable costs incurred in the collection of a *Fi-Fa* are recoverable before any proceeds are applied to 'knockdown' the judgment. This includes towing/storage fees, fees for issuance of the writ, fees for the placing of a second lien on an automobile title, Sheriff's fees, etc.

DOCUMENTATION OF THE SEIZURE

Plaintiff should keep an accurate and detailed record of these expenses. Proper documentation will help to establish the reasonableness of the expenses and to ensure their recovery. The Sheriff's levy officer can apprise the plaintiff of the details.

Circumstances may be such, that plaintiff may wish to photograph the condition of the property at the time of levy, thus documenting the condition of the levied property at the time it was seized. Documentation of condition can only serve to protect the plaintiff from false accusations. With the increasing availability of relatively inexpensive camcorders, digital cameras, etc., it is becoming increasingly easier to document your efforts.

The levying officer may wish to document the presence of everyone that was present at the time of the levy; other officers, tow truck drivers, plaintiff, plaintiff's attorney, movers, defendant, defendant's family members, defendant's employees, etc. Remember, documentation can never be over-emphasized and can only serve to protect the plaintiff and the levying officer in the execution of his lawful duties.

CONSTITUTIONAL PROTECTIONS

CONSTITUTIONAL RIGHTS OF DEFENDANT

Under the **Fourteenth Amendment to the United State Constitution**, an individual should be secure in their right to life, liberty and their property. A levy under law abridges this right. Due caution should be exercised not to infringe upon any Constitutional rights guaranteed the defendant when executing levy.

The levy officer should make every effort to try and appear as unbiased as possible while bearing in mind that he is acting as an agent of the Sheriff, on behalf of the court, to benefit the plaintiff, while protecting the rights of the defendant. It may be that the events surrounding the levy may have to be placed in testimony before the court if the levy officer is traversed.

The **Fourth Amendment to the United States Constitution** greatly limits to what lengths the levy officer may go in attempting to search for something upon which to levy while at the premises of the defendant's residence or business. At no time does the writ allow free rein to search at will. This is why the plaintiff should have done the pre-levy legwork to determine what property the defendant may have that would e subject to levy.

Be very sure that the property seized belongs to the defendant in *Fi-Fa*. The fact that a defendant is in possession of certain property is not always *prima facia* evidence of ownership. It may be sufficient to permit seizure, but may possibly be released by the courts, back to the defendant, when the proper action has been filed. If there is a potential question of ownership, consult with the county attorney.

You should document any and all claims by the defendant as to any third party ownership. The assistance of a second officer with an audio recorder would be very helpful. The occasion may arise later whereby the defendant tries to substantiate the claim with different information. The conflicting facts may be sufficient to deny the claim, citing it as an attempt to defraud.

O.C.G.A. 9-3-90 through **O.C.G.A. 9-13-106** covers third party claims to the property seized. There have been occasions where the defendant has claimed their property belonged to a third person. Then this third person refuses to become involved in the charade and the defendant is left to try and cover up their efforts at circumventing the seizure.

The levy officer is always in the middle. Virtually everything that transpires in the course of a levy and seizure is ultimately the responsibility of the levying officer. While personal safety is paramount, it is foremost that the execution of the writ be performed without the infringement upon the rights of the defendant, while pursuing the rights of the plaintiff in the collection of the judgment.

The levy officer should always bear in mind that he is acting as an agent of the sheriff, on behalf of the court and at the court's direction, to benefit the plaintiff, while protecting the rights of the defendant. Doing so will assure that the defendant's rights under the **Fourth and Fourteenth Amendments to the U.S. Constitution** are protected.

A judgment arising out of a dispossessory action has one advantage. The timely scheduling of the eviction could assist in the determination of property upon which to levy. The plaintiff may obtain their writ immediately upon the rendering of judgment and then execute a levy during the eviction process. This assumes that the defendant would have property that would be subject to levy.

EXCEPTIONS TO LEVY AND SALE

CONSTITUTIONAL EXEMPTIONS

44-13-1 through **44-13-87** and **44-14-100 (1981) O.C.G.A.** sets forth the constitutional and statutory exemptions from levy. No part of the uniform or equipment of any member of the duly organized militia, officer nor enlisted personnel, is subject to levy. For property to be exempt under homestead exemption, an itemized list must be properly filed with the Probate Court.

Realty or personalty or both of a debtor in the amount of $5,000.00 is exempt from levy and sale with certain exceptions. Commonly referred to as a homestead exemption, the Georgia legislature's 1983 session made numerous changes to **Chapter 13 of Title 44**, including deletion of the term homestead.

This exemption is now referred to as a constitutional exemption, since it is authorized by the Constitution. Such property referred to under this section is exempt from levy and sale when set apart in accordance with the Code except for:

(**1**.) Taxes;

(**2**.) The purchase money of the property;

(**3**.) Labor performed on, or materials furnished for, the property; or

(**4**.) Removal of encumbrances thereon.

Under Georgia law, both real and personal property may be set apart; however, if cash is set aside, it must be invested in personal property selected by the applicant under the direction of the Judge of the Probate Court and a schedule of the property must be filed with the Judge of Probate Court.

The person seeking the benefit of the exemptions provided for by the Constitution must apply to the Judge of the Probate Court of the county in which he resides, by petition stating:

(**1**.) The debtor for whom the exemption is claimed;

(**2**.) The names and ages of the minor children and dependents of the debtor.

(**3**.) What and whose property the exemptions are claimed.

The petition must comply with all existing laws for the setting apart and valuation of exemptions. The individual seeking this protection must create this petition and the property schedule for presentation to the Probate Judge. The petition must be accompanied by a schedule containing:

(1.) A detailed and accurate description of all real and personal property belonging to the person from whose estate the exemptions is to be made, so that interested persons may know exactly what is exempted and what is not.

(2.) A list of the person's creditors and their post office addresses, if known, which must be sworn to by the applicant or his agent.

The debtor claiming the Constitutional exemption benefit is obligated to act in good faith. Any willful fraud in the schedule of property will void the judgment allowing the exemption. Such property is subject to just and legal debts at the time the fraud was perpetrated.

Failure to comply with these requirements in the original petition or subsequent amendments requires a dismissal by the Judge of the Probate Court. If the debtor applying for exemption fails to make a detailed and complete showing of all their property, the judgment allowing the exemption is null and void. A creditor contesting that judgment and that the schedule is incomplete has the right of appeal to the Superior Court.

STATUTORY EXEMPTIONS

Any debtor, who is a natural person, may exempt for the purposes of bankruptcy, specific items and amounts of property under the statutory exemptions. **(O.C.G.A. 44-3-100)** formerly referred to as a pony homestead or short homestead. A debtor is not permitted to avail themselves of the benefits of both the Constitutional and the statutory exemptions.

The debtor must choose which type of exemption they wish to claim. If there is a widow and or child of an intestate insolvent estate, the statutory exemptions may also be claimed by the intestate.

The Judge of the Probate Court in receiving and recording the schedule is merely performing a ministerial act. The debtor is solely responsible for a true and accurate schedule of assets. There is no duty upon the Judge of Probate for the accuracy of the asset schedule. The Judge of Probate is not obligated further in the filing of this exemption.

A short list of exemptions from levy:

1. ~ personal property set aside as a homestead.

2. ~ property set aside for a year's support of a widow.

3. ~ Choses in Actions. (exceptions are shares of stock)

4. ~ you can not levy on promissory notes.

5. ~ you can not levy on growing crops that are not mature.

6. ~ communications equipment used in interstate commerce.

7. ~ public or quasi-public property.

8. ~ consignment property.

9. ~ school property.

10. ~ uniform and equipment of member of Militia/Military/ National Guard/Reserve

11. ~ most leased property.

12. ~ wages. (The plaintiff in *Fi-Fa* must attach this by way of garnishment.)

13. ~ property that has been transferred by a debtor to someone else prior to the judgment.

14. ~ money in the hands of the Sheriff that was paid by the defendant to satisfy a specific execution.

15. ~ property that is in the custody of the law. (Property that has been seized as contraband or already subject to a prior levy.)

16. ~ 'tools of the trade'. These are the tools a defendant employs to actually earn his living; i.e., carpenter, mechanic, mason, etc.

BANKRUPTCY

A protection provided through the federal courts is the filing of bankruptcy. The filing of bankruptcy by the defendant in **Fi-Fa** automatically stays all actions, pending further order by the bankruptcy judge. A bankruptcy is filed with the Clerk of the United States Bankruptcy Court. A schedule of creditors will reflect all creditors affected by the bankruptcy. In most cases, if a creditor is not listed on this schedule, their judgment or debt remains unaffected.

A bankruptcy, affecting the Sheriff's Sale, may be filed anytime right up to the moment of the sale. This places a stay on all judicial proceedings. This stay affects any stage of the process including the judicial sale. Notification of the Sheriff must take place prior to the completion of the sale for the stay to be valid. Failure of proper and timely notification to all judgment creditors and the Sheriff of the bankruptcy filing could result in a failure to protect the defendant's position. It is in the defendant's interest to follow through on all steps and see that everyone is properly notified.

In the case where a bankruptcy has been set aside or denied, speedy action on the part of the judgment plaintiff could result in a successful levy. The defendant has a waiting period before being able to file for bankruptcy protection again. An alert plaintiff can successfully levy during this period and achieve the judicial sale. There are harsh penalties for the defendant for attempts to use the bankruptcy courts for the purpose of an attempt to defraud creditors.

REPLEVY BOND

In the appropriate circumstances, a replevy bond, also known as a forthcoming bond, may be posted by the defendant in *Fi-Fa*, allowing the defendant the use and possession of the property pending a hearing before the court issuing the judgment. This is not always an automatic tight, but a privilege that the defendant must request from the court to receive. The court may deny this privilege without prejudice.

O.C.G.A. 9-3-90 through **O.C.G.A. 9-13-106** covers claims made by third parties to the property seized. **O.C.G.A. 9-13-91** asserts that the person claiming the property levyed on, or his agent or his attorney, shall give food bond to the Sheriff or other levying officer, with good and sufficient security in a sum not larger than <u>double the amount</u> of the execution levied, made payable to the plaintiff in execution. This bond should be made returnable to the judge or magistrate issuing the writ.

Where the property levyed on is of less value than the execution, the amount of the bond shall be double the value of the property levyed upon, at a reasonable valuation to be judged by the levying officer, conditioned to pay the plaintiff in execution all damages which the jury on the trial of the claim may assess against the person claiming the property in case it appears that the claim was made for the purpose of delay only.

O.C.G.A. 9-13-94(a) In all cases where a levy is made upon property that is claimed by a third person and the person desires the possession thereof, it shall be the duty of the sheriff or other levying officer to take bond, made payable to the sheriff with good security for a sum equal to double the value of the property levied on to be estimated by the levying officer, for the delivery of the property at the time and place of sale, provided the property so levied upon shall be found subject to the execution. However, it shall not be lawful to require or take a forthcoming bond for real estate.

O.C.G.A. 9-13-94(b) states that when bond and security have been given as provided in this Code section, it shall be the duty of the sheriff or other levying officer to leave the property in the possession of the claimant. In the event that the claimant or his security fails to deliver the property after it has been found to be subject to execution, the bond shall be made recoverable in any court having cognizance of the same. This amounts to forfeiture of the posted bond collateral.

APPLICABLE CASE LAWS

The amount of case law involving levys and seizures is severely limited. There is great reliance on *Old English Common Law*. The levy officer should not rely solely on the plaintiff's attorney to properly or completely research applicable statutory or case law. Not necessarily that they would attempt anything improper, but the levy officer is subjecting themselves to possible liability based on another's ability or expertise in researching the material.

It should be kept in mind that not many attorneys have experience in the area of levys and seizures. The levy officer is not expected to know all that there is to know about seizures. This is one of the reasons the county has someone on retainer, appointed as county attorney.

It is always the best policy to err on the side of caution. Always rely on your instincts. If any given set of circumstances do not feel comfortable, seek immediate guidance and direction from your supervisor, county attorney and judges. **Do not proceed** without some direction from your superiors or some judicial authority. Prior preparation can avoid potential liability. Don't take unnecessary risks.

As with most anything judicial, the final word is ultimately the interpretation by your particular court. If this interpretation differs substantially from what you have been trained, taught, or learned through your department's accepted practice, do not hesitate to consult your county attorney. Once a dispute has been resolved, document your efforts and the decision you receive. Bring your superiors into the process. Remember, liability extends upward. They want and need to be kept aware of any potential liability risks.

Do not risk civil action upon yourself without proper authorization from your superiors. Anything beyond this would most likely be decided upon appeal to the court of proper jurisdiction. The levy officer is never likely to be totally absolved from the risk of liability. It is a good policy to make every attempt to limit this risk as much as possible. When executing a *writ of execution*, the officer is afforded some protection by the issuing judge's immunity.

RELATED
JUDICIAL DECISIONS

Entry of levy is the officer's declaration and documentation that he has seized the property for the purposes of judicial sale. **Head v. Lee 203 Ga. 191, 45 S.D. 2d 666 (1947)**

Entry of levy should be signed by the levying officer in order that it may be authenticated as the official act of the officer. **Jones v. Easley, 53 Ga. 454 (1873)**

Where entry has not been signed, the officer may amend it by adding his signature. **Sharp v. Kennedy, 50 Ga. 208 (1873)**

Interest of defendant must be plainly set forth in entry of levy. **Harden v. Bell, 212 Ga. 711, 95 S.E. 2d 375 (1956)**

The interest in the property intended to be seized and sold must be defined or specified in levy, and not set out generally as an interest, or as in the interest of the defendant in the property. **Bledsoe v. Willingham, 62 Ga. 550 (1879); Thornton v. Ferguson, 133 Ga. 825, 67 S.E. 97, 134 AM. St. R. 226 (1910)**

It is not sufficient that the entry recites that 'the interest' or 'all the interest' of the defendant. **Harden v. Bell, 21 Ga. 711, 95 S.E. 2d375 (1956)**

The officer levying a . . . . . Fi-Fa Can exercise a reasonable discretion as to the sufficiency of the property to pay the execution, and should be allowed a reasonable margin between the value of the property levied upon and the amount of the . . . . . . **Fi-Fa Planters Bank v. Georgia Loan & Trust Co., 160 Ga. 107 (1,b) (127 S.E. 413) and citations.**

SAFETY PRACTICES

SAFETY CONCERNS AND CONSIDERATIONS

Diligence and caution are of prime concern in the performance and pursuit of executing a levy. The levy officer should endeavor to exercise every possible caution in executing the levy. The prudent officer should consult every available source for information before attempting to execute a levy. Protecting oneself from serious injury or death is as critical as the concerns for possible civil liability. Express consideration for officer safety should be paramount.

Never assume that the levy will take place without incident. Be as prepared as possible for events of violence. Experienced officers are well aware that events can to a complete and total reversal in the blink of an eye. The old cliché of *'forewarned is forearmed'* comes to mind. Complacency and negligence can result in disaster.

Before setting out to execute the levy, ascertain all pertinent and relevant information that you possibly can from the plaintiff about the defendant. A substantial amount of research must be conducted in the successful execution of every levy. Interview the plaintiff. Review any available records of arrest of the defendant. Take an extra moment to contemplate risk/threat assessment of the potential conditions that might be present during the levy attempt.

Allot sufficient time for the execution of the levy so as to not be rushed. It may be another cliché', but the old adage; *'haste makes waste'* is very true. Try to ascertain potential risk factors such as the defendant's temperament, presence of potentially vicious animals, if defendant is known to possess a weapon, how many employees might be present at the business site, etc. These along with other existing factors such as the time of day the levy might be executed, light conditions, pedestrian/vehicular traffic, customers, bystanders, weather conditions, etc., should all be taken into consideration.

Executing and perfecting a successful levy is more of an art or skill, than a science. Knowing people and how they tend to react can be just as important as knowledge of the law. An experienced and knowledgeable levy officer can avert any number of obstacles that might be encountered through advance research and preparation.

No one is able to anticipate every potential pitfall, but the levy officer should make every effort to be as prepared as they possibly may. Cognizances of potential pitfalls are tools in trade for an experienced and responsible levy officer. The strict adherence to the statutes is mandatory. Any questionable circumstances should be referred to the county attorney for clarification and resolution.

It may be such that a check for any outstanding warrants and of the defendant's arrest record may be warranted before attempting to execute levy. A check with fellow officers for any prior contact and interaction with the defendant might also be advisable. Some of the most trivial information may be the most beneficial.

Plaintiff should be cautioned against arguing with or entering into a confrontation with the defendant. Provocation of an altercation could possibly result in the injury and/or arrest of both parties. An arrogant defendant tends to provoke verbal attacks from the plaintiff, at the very least. Be careful.

Arrogance on the part of the defendant can sometimes lead to locating property on which to levy. This arrogance can most times be tolerated. Arrogance is usually present in a braggart that just can not stand to keep quiet and just has to drop clues as to *'how smart he is'* and how you'll never find anything on which to levy. Simply stay alert for clues that could lead to the possible whereabouts of assets.

CONTROL OF
THE LEVY

Always attempt to maintain control of the situation. If plaintiff refuses to maintain proper demeanor, ask them to remove themselves from the scene until they are needed. The levy officer should make the plaintiff aware that the levy process is not an opportunity for revenge.

Make it clear that the levy officer is to be in charge at all times. If the situation deteriorates to the point of becoming dangerous, the levy attempt should be aborted. If it appears that the situation could become volatile, additional officer assistance should be requested.

Do not assume that because the encounter begins without confrontation that everything will proceed without incident. As any experienced officer can attest, things can go bad in an instant. The least provocation may trigger tempers to flare in an instant.

Vigilance is absolutely mandatory and personal safety is of prime consideration. Be especially cautious of the defendant that vehemently denies that you have anything to fear from them. *Stay alert and on guard*.

CONCEALMENT OF ASSETS/ FRAUDULENT CONVEYANCES

In some cases the defendant in *Fi-Fa* may have moved or transferred their assets to others in an attempt to prevent collection or levy. These transfers of ownership should be properly recorded to be legal and binding. The transference of assets to avoid the possibility of levy can potentially be set aside.

In many cases these attempts at concealment are obvious and lame. In these cases it may be possible to go ahead and seize the property. Check with your county attorney first.

In certain cases it may require the assistance of an attorney to cancel these transfers. In the case of a corporation it may require the 'piercing of the corporate veil' and allow the collection of the judgment from a corporation's shareholders or other potential assets.

If the fraudulent transaction takes place in regard to a bankruptcy filing, sanctions in the United States Bankruptcy Court could result.

Any fraudulent actions are of the gravest concern and should be reported immediately to the proper authority, usually the Bankruptcy Trustee.

If the discovery process establishes some indication of fraudulent conveyance, the plaintiff may file a petition in equity to set aside the conveyance, invalidating the transfer. **(O.C.G.A. 18-2-3)** If such petition is filed, it should be brought against the transferor and the transferee.

In some cases it may possibly even be a criminal act to attempt to conceal assets in an effort to defraud. In these cases it may become necessary to involve the criminal investigators and the District Attorney's office. It would be best to consult with the District Attorney before the filing of criminal charges.

ALTERNATIVE METHODS OF COLLECTION

These alternatives are not, nor are they meant to be, comprehensive, nor all inclusive. They are the most common and widely used. Separate research could possibly ascertain even more obscure and arcane methods from antiquity that may still be applicable.

GARNISHMENTS

This particular judicial proceeding is valuable to those civil plaintiffs that have been awarded a money judgment against insolvent defendants. A garnishment permits the plaintiff to satisfy their judgment by asserting their claim directly against money or property owed to the defendant by a third party or an employer.

The plaintiff, after the issuance of the summons of garnishment and not more than three business days after the service of the summons of garnishment on the garnishee, shall cause written notice to be delivered to the defendant by the plaintiff or his attorney at law by first class mail or service of notice by the sheriff.

The plaintiff may pursue a garnishment of the defendant's employer, bank account or any other funds found to be due the defendant in *Fi-Fa* pursuant to **O.C.G.A.** **18-4-64** while simultaneously attempting to levy under *Fi-Fa*. The garnishment of a defendant's bank account would be a one time event. The garnishment of the defendant's paycheck or wages would be a continuing garnishment.

The author has experienced a case where the husband, a very highly experienced welder in great demand, stating that he owned nothing, claiming that everything belonged to his wife and all vehicles were registered in her name and that he worked for her. After speaking with the plaintiff, a garnishment was issued and served on the wife as the defendant's employer. They paid off the *Fi-Fa* to prevent her from having to do the paperwork connected with a garnishment.

There are important differences between an attachment and a garnishment, although they may appear to be somewhat similar. The essential differences are;

1. - In garnishment, the plaintiff files an action against a third party that owes   money or holds money or property to his judgment debtor.   In an attachment the   plaintiff files an action against the debtor.

2. - A garnishment does not require the seizure of property. An attachment requires that the Sheriff seize property of the defendant to satisfy the debt.

3. - A garnishment may be issued after notice is given to the defendant and a   hearing will be conducted on the merits of the garnishment petition. The   garnishee has 45 days to respond to the summons of garnishment. An attachment does not require a preliminary judgment on the merits of a plaintiff's case.

GARNISHMENT IN ATTACHMENT

A garnishment in attachment combines the elements of a garnishment and an attachment. There is no pre-existing judgment required, as in an attachment. What is necessary is for the defendant to:

1. -reside outside the limits of the state of Georgia; or

2. - be actually removing or about to move outside the jurisdiction of the state of Georgia; or

3. - be causing removal of his property outside the limits of the state of Georgia; or

4. - is transferring, has transferred, or is about to transfer property to defraud or evade his creditors; or

5. - is insolvent.

As in garnishment proceedings, this action is issued against a third party.

NE EXEAT

Ne exeat is a writ issued to prevent a person from leaving the jurisdiction of the court. It forbids the defendant to move themselves and/or remove particularly designated property from the court's reach, where there would be a failure of justice or a hindrance of the court's judgment.

The defendant may relieve this restraint by posting bond with good security for double the amount of the defendant's claim. The judge granting the issuance of the writ may require a larger bond if, in his discretion, circumstances indicate or warrant the necessity.

EXECUTION OF LEVY
AND GARNISHMENT

To garnishee and execute levy simultaneously would require that the judgment to be of a considerable amount, so as to not over-levy or over-collect the judgment. Any questions or concerns should be expressed to the levying officer. In the event the response should fall in the category of legal advice, it would be wise to seek legal counsel. In the overwhelming majority of cases, there is usually not a problem.

Writs may be obtained out of a judgment rendered for the failure to answer or respond to a garnishment. This writ would then be issued against the garnishee. The garnishee would then be subject to all collection actions as would any other defendant in *Fi-Fa.*

Rickey E. Tumlin

EMPLOYMENT OF AGENTS
FOR COLLECTION

In certain circumstances, the plaintiff may elect to employ an agent to act on their behalf. This may be a relative, friend, collection agency or attorney. There are people that are commercially available that act as collection agents. The plaintiff would be wise to limit the use of an outside agent for the collection of their judgment.

Under all circumstances the plaintiff should ensure that the agent employed is reputable, dependable and reliable. The plaintiff could potentially be held liable for actions performed the agent in the execution of collection.

The levy officer should require a notarized affidavit of power of attorney authorizing any agent, other than an actual attorney at law, to act on behalf of behalf of the plaintiff. This power of attorney should be placed in the Clerk's case file. It would be wise on the part of the levy officer to be sure that the plaintiff is aware that they could potentially be subject to any liability incurred by an agent acting on their behalf.

TRANSFER OF
THE JUDGMENT

The plaintiff may assign or transfer their judgment to another party. There are firms and individuals that purchase judgments and *Fi-Fa's* on a speculative basis at a discounted amount. **O.C.G.A. 9-12-21** permits a judgment plaintiff to transfer or assign the judgment to a third party for bona fide and valuable considerations.

This assignment should be recorded on the **G.E.D.** In cases where the plaintiff is in need of an immediate return on the judgment, this may be a viable option. Under no circumstance should the officer endorse or veto this action.

Fraudulent assignments or transfers for the purpose of collection are to be avoided. Thus the plaintiff assigns their interest to the purchaser under only the most proper of circumstances. This assignment should then be entered on the **G.E.D.** This will properly record the assignees assertion of right to collect. A new *Fi-Fa* will be issued reflecting the assignee as the payee of proceeds.

PERFECTING JUDGMENT AS SECOND LIEN

Upon written request, the **Georgia Division of Motor Vehicle Services** will provide the necessary forms to have the judgment recorded as a second lien on the title of defendant's motor vehicle. Once the forms have been completed, they should be submitted, with a copy of the *Fi-Fa* and money order for the appropriate fee, via registered mail to the entity holding the certificate of motor vehicle title. **(O.C.G.A. 40-3-38b)**

The entity holding the certificate of title is required by law to comply and cooperate in the perfection of the second lien. This is a method of collection that involves little or no opportunity of confrontation, excellent probability of the collection of the judgment, with a minimum of personal risk, effort and expense.

REGISTRATION AND LICENSING OF MOTOR VEHICLES

O.C.G.A. 40-2-130c

The motor vehicle registration records which the Commissioner is required to maintain under this code section or any other provision are exempt fro the provisions of any law of this state requiring that such records be open for public inspection, provided however, that the record of any particular motor vehicle be made available for inspection by the following:

(1.) Any law enforcement officer for official law enforcement investigations as certified by the commanding officer of the law enforcement agency making any such request.

(2.) The owner of the vehicle.

(3.) Any judgment creditor of the owner of the vehicle upon presentation of an *original writ of fieri facias*.

(4.) Any individual or an authorized agent or representative of such individual that has been involved in a motor vehicle accident, either as an operator of a motor vehicle, a passenger in a motor vehicle or as a pedestrian.

(5.) Any licensed dealer of new or used motor vehicles.

(6.) Any person for the purposes of a manufacturer's recall.

(7.) Any tax collector, tax receiver or tax commissioner.

(8.) Georgia Environmental Protection Agency Director or his designee.

(9.) Wrecker operators and impound lot owners **(O.C.G.A. 40-11-2,3,5).**

The <u>Commissioner</u> of the **Georgia Department of Motor Vehicle Services** may, if necessary, promulgate reasonable rules and regulations outlining any additional circumstances, under which warrant that such records shall be open for public inspection.

PERFECTING THE LEVY

ENTRY OF LEVY
ON PROCESS

O.C.G.A. 9-11-12 requires that the levying officer shall make precise entry of the levy on the process, by virtue of which levy is made and this entry shall plainly describe the property that has been seized and the amount of the interest of the defendant therein. This entry can be made by hand, by the affixing of a rubber stamped form or, if provided, in the form pre-printed on the Fi-Fa at the time of issuance.

An exact and accurate itemized inventory of the items seized must be duly entered upon the *Fi-Fa*, giving all the pertinent information including the make, model and serial numbers and degree of ownership. It should disclose with reasonable certainty what the degree of that interest is. Entry of the day, date and hour of the levy should also be recorded.

Entry of '*knockdown*' should also be made on the *Fi-Fa*, reflecting buyer, sale price, Sheriff's commission, other legitimate costs and fees, net proceeds and the amount of principal after knockdown. "Knockdown" is to dispose of property to a bidder at an auction sale, with the proceeds of sale applied to the costs of sale and then to the judgment.

SHERIFF'S SALE (JUDICIAL SALE)

STATUTORY REGULATIONS

The Sheriff's Sale is to be conducted on the court house steps, unless another location is designated by written order of the *Senior Superior Court Judge* of that county (**O.C.G.A. 9-13-161c**). Subject to certain exceptions for legal holidays, Sheriff's sales are to be held on the first Tuesday of the month (**O.C.G.A.9-13-161a**).

Pursuant to **O.C.G.A. 9-13-160b**, the legal hours of sale are from 10:00 am till 4:00 pm. If the sale is begun by 4:00 pm, this does not preclude the sale extending beyond 4:00 pm by a reasonable period of time.

15-16-21b O.C.G.A. sets the commission rate to be collected by the Sheriff from proceeds of Sheriff's Sales. These fees, amongst others, are set by the legislature and are standard and consistent state wide. Fees collected are deposited into the General Fund of the county and disbursed according to law.

THE LEGAL ADVVERTISEMENT

O.C.G.A. 15-16-10(a) (4) states that the seized property must be published in a Sheriff's Notice of Sale in the legal classifieds section (usual heading is SALE UNDER POWER) of the legal organ. The plaintiff and the levy officer should make careful note to proof-read the legal advertisement. Better yet, ask someone that you trust to proof-read it, too. Then, once it is printed, proof-read the published advertisement immediately. Accuracy is definitely paramount.

The first insertion of the legal advertisement is traditionally agreed to be the responsibility of the newspaper, unless it is the obvious mistake of the person placing the advertisement. Any subsequent incorrect insertions are the responsibility of the advertiser, regardless of who is at fault. It was our county attorney's opinion that as long as the advertisement was corrected by the final insertion, it should not affect the validity of the Sheriff's Judicial Sale.

If the inaccuracy in the advertisement is critical enough, this could void the advertisement, resulting in delays of the sale or in the extreme possibly void a sale that may have already taken place. The plaintiff should be required to pay for the legal advertisement in advance, unless prior arrangements are made by the plaintiff with the legal organ.

The notice of sale must be published once per week for the four weeks immediately prior to the sale date in the legal organ of the jurisdiction. With some exceptions for legal holidays, the Sheriff's Sale has to take place the first Tuesday of the month immediately following the publication **(O.C.G.A. 9-13-161a)**. The legal organ is determined jointly by the Sheriff, Clerk of Superior Court and the Judge of Probate.

As a general rule, Sheriff's sales generate only a limited amount of interest, attendance and participation. Generally, property sold at a judicial sale or Sheriff's Sale will only garner about **15** to **50** cents on the dollar of its current market value. As an overall rule, it may be even less.

The sale officer must be cautious and attempt to generate the best price possible for the property. In this respect, the levy officer is acting as an agent for the defendant in being responsible for obtaining the best price possible for the property. As is the case with most everything, there are some exceptions as to what generates the best price.

As an exception to the rule, there are some items that will generate extraordinary interest and bring bids well above its intrinsic or fair market value. There is never any way to gauge or anticipate this interest. Sheriff's sales are subject to the principle of supply and demand. There is no accounting for what may appeal to a bidder's tastes or desires.

The levy officer will find that the Sheriff's Sale will pick up some regular attendees with no interest whatsoever in purchase, but will attempt ridiculously low bids in the event there is minimal or no interest generated by the sale. This is generally a bid totally out of proportion with the value of the property.

In this event, it is incumbent upon the Sheriff to withdraw the property from sale and proceed accordingly. In the event of an absolute sale, there is no alternative but to sell the property for the highest bid acquired. This is not always a good policy in the event of items of exceptional value.

CONDUCTING
THE SHERIFF'S SALE

PRE-SALE
PREPARATION

The seized property should be made available for examination by the public prior to the sale. Depending on the circumstances and logistics of the storage, this may be the morning of the sale or other times convenient to the levy officer. When there are restrictive circumstances or conditions on such items that may be in storage, by making appointment with the storage facility.

Naturally, not all levied property can be physically present for the sale. The individual departmental policy may affect the method that the location of the sale is determined.

There may be occasions where the weather, vehicular traffic, community events, etc., may affect the location of the sale. Always try to make allowances for most any contingency. Such may affect the validity of the sale.

Again, the levy officer may wish to consult with the county attorney in the event of questionable circumstances. The Senior Superior Court Judge or Chief Superior Court Judge of the county may issue an order setting alternative sites for judicial sales.

Conditions may be such that you would want the sale to be held at the property's storage location or in the case of real estate at the site of the property itself. This is not necessary for the sale to be lawful, but may help to increase the amount bid. You would then read off the legal ad at the court house or lawfully designated place of sale and then announce that you will adjourn to the announced location.

If the judicial sale is conducted at another location, document on the *Fi-Fa* The date, time and location the sale took place. The judicial sale can legally take place at its traditional site, with the property never being removed from its storage location.

It is obligatory on the part of the Sheriff to secure as good a price possible on the property sold. If a better price can be obtained by the selling of the property a piece at the time, it should be done so. If interest can not be generated by this method, it is permissible to auction the property in bulk lots.

The key to conducting a successful sale is order and organization. Announce to the crowd that complete silence must be maintained during the bidding process. That when they wish to bid, for them to speak loudly and clearly.

The officer acting as auctioneer should also speak clearly and distinctly, with sufficient volume to reach all the bidders present. Succinctly let the bidders know that if you don't acknowledge the bid by repeating it, you have not heard their bid and effectively, they have not bid.

Some prospective bidders tend to overstep their position and have to be told explicitly how the sale is going to transpire. The sale officer should not hesitate to exert their authority and let it be known that the sale officer is in charge.

It is seldom necessary, but the sale officer has the authority to eject anyone not complying with his directives to be able to maintain order. The sale officer is the supreme authority in the conducting of the sale.

DISCLAIMERS

Prior to the reading of the legal advertisement is the time to make any and all disclaimers and announcements pertaining to the sale. Some examples of such announcements:

> — all items are sold as is.

> — all sale items are subject to any prior outstanding liens, known or unknown.

— all sales are final

— announce whether the sale is to be an absolute sale or reserve sale.

— exemptions from sales tax must be documented by buyer's sales tax exempt   certificate number.

— payment must be in cash or other certified funds.

— reserve the right to decide if to be absolute sale or set minimum opening bid.

— reserve the right to set minimum bid increments.

— reserve the right to refuse/decline any and all bids.

— reserve right to remove any and all items from sale.

— sales tax must be charged on all sales of personal property.

— sales tax can not be charged on real estate sales.

— used bedding may not be sold (i.e., mattresses, box springs, sheets).

The levy officer may want to review this list prior to each sale. There may be some that he wants to use for one sale and then leave out on others. That is the beauty of your pronouncements. The ones that are recited for that particular sale are the ones that apply. The levy and sale officer should document those that are used.

SCRIPTING THE SALE

If the Sheriff, or his designee for the sale, wishes to write a script for the sale, he is welcome to do so, even encouraged. This would ensure that all relevant and required points were covered in the conducting of the sale. This script should include all descriptive information, topics of interest related to the property, disclaimers, and etcetera. Should the sale officer suffer from a slight case of 'stage fright', this would help to overcome the problem.

This could be important in the event that the sale officer was called to task over a particular point or issue. The officer could refer to his script and point out that it was read aloud, word for word and leave no room for aspersion. This protection would also hold true in the reading of the legal advertisement. Having been read aloud, word for word, leaves little room for allegations of impropriety.

Make the announcement of any and all other pertinent information, such as one-half undivided interest in real property. This would mean that the purchaser would have a co-owner and would not have total ownership in the property. This would leave the purchaser to try to buy out the other owner, if so desired and the co-owner was willing to sell.

Such circumstances might require the consultation of the county attorney. This situation would most likely arise only if the co-owner willingly permit's the levy and sale. This could occur if the co-owner is also the plaintiff or was of a mind to part with their share of ownership as in a lien holder situation.

The auctioneer should have all the necessary information at his fingertips pertaining to the items at sale. Information such as; engine size, mileage, type of transmission, etc., on an automobile, the length, hull material, horsepower on the engine, inboard-outboard engine, etc., on a boat.

The sale officer should try to anticipate any potential questions. The pronouncement of this specific information helps the prospective bidders to know exactly on what they are bidding and to generate the best price for the property.

If a minimum bid is not required, the costs, fees and other expenses should be paid and collected up front from the plaintiff prior to the sale. In the case of an *'absolute'* sale, failure to do so could leave you scrabbling to recover the costs after the sale. Caution should be exercised so as to not leave the county liable for any costs incurred.

If a minimum bid is required, make sure that it is set sufficient to cover any and all costs, fees and expenses incurred related to the levy and sale. Normally, but not always, the plaintiff in ***Fi-Fa*** will elect to bid the minimum bid.

The auctioneer should have an employee assisting in the sale by recording the bids and taking down the bidders' information, a second employee collecting the monies and writing receipts. This leaves the auctioneer free to focus on the bidding and the bidders.

It would be preferable for the levying officer to be present so as to be available for immediate consultation in the event of any questions. The plaintiff does not assist in the conducting of the Sheriff's Sale in any manner whatsoever.

PURCHASER RISK

The doctrine of *'Caveat Emptor'* (Latin for *'let the buyer beware'*) applies to a Sheriff's Sale. The doctrine, as applied in this instance, is loosely defined as <u>purchasers buy at their own risk</u>. This concept also encompasses land sales.

A purchaser at a tax sale falls with the *Caveat Emptor* doctrine. The Sheriff should make this clear, prior to the actual conducting of the sale. This should be one of the disclaimers announced prior to the start of the sale.

A purchaser at a Sheriff's Sale has every right to presume that a public officer, being known to possess the power to levy and sell, has taken every step required under the law, pursuant to which he is conducting his sale. A purchaser is bound only to determine that the officer has lawful authority to sell and is proceeding under prescribed rules of law. A purchaser has the right to presume that, upon purchase at a legal sale, full and clear title of ownership shall be bestowed by the Sheriff.

A bidder misled by statements calculated to mislead as to the condition or identity of the property, real or personal, is not bound to comply with his bid. The sale officer should allow a moment for any potential questions before beginning the sale.

THE AUCTION

SHERIFF AS AGENT
FOR DEFENDANT

The Sheriff or his lawful designee, acting as auctioneer, is bound to accept any and all bids, unless he knows that the party making the bid is insolvent and unable to pay for the property. The Sheriff should exercise care in the descriptive terms used in the presentation of goods for bid.

A Sheriff's Sale should be conducted in a lawful manner such that will secure the best price for the property sold. The sanctions of the Sheriff or levying officer in the levy process under most all appearances look as if he is acting only as an agent for the plaintiff.

The levy/sale officer should remember that he is also acting as agent for the defendant. In the course of conducting the sale, the sale officer has the duty to try to raise as much cash proceeds as possible towards the satisfaction of the judgment while depriving the defendant of as little property as possible.

If the property can be divided, so as to bring a better price, the officer should do so. If not, then it should be sold in a bulk lot. It should never appear that the Sheriff is showing any sort of deference or preferential treatment to any particular bidder. A Sheriff cannot sell more of the defendant's property than is necessary to satisfy the execution. Any incidental overage must be refunded to the defendant.

Neither the Sheriff, nor his deputies, nor his employees, are permitted to purchase at their own sale, nor should they *procure* anyone to do so on their behalf. **(O.C.G.A. 15-116-18)** This would include friends, spouses, in-laws or other relatives. There is no provision for exception under this statute. Even the appearance of impropriety should be avoided. Bear in mind that the Sheriff is ultimately responsible for the actions of his designees.

BIDDING BY
THE PLAINTIFF

The judgment plaintiff may elect to bid on the property offered at the Sheriff's Sale. In doing so, the judgment amount may be applied towards the purchase, up to the entire value of the judgment. The plaintiff would then pay only the cash amount necessary to cover the sales tax, Sheriff's commission and other fees and the difference between the bid and the judgment, if plaintiff's bid should exceed the judgment. Excess proceeds of the sale, if any, must be refunded by the Sheriff to the defendant.

BIDDING BY
THE DEFENDANT

The judgment defendant may wish to bid on the property and may legally elect to do so. In the event that the defendant should be present and purchase the property, this is entirely possible, legal and proper.

Plaintiff may wait until the payment is collected and then, in the event that the sale did not generate sufficient funds to satisfy the judgment, direct the Sheriff to levy once again on the property, thus giving the plaintiff two stabs at recovering sufficient funds to satisfy the judgment from the same defendant property.

In the legal vernacular, two bites of the apple. Should this ever occur, the same procedure must be followed again in the procedure of advertisement and sale of the property. During his career, the author has actually had this occur, not just once, but with three different defendants.

The sale officer should not deny the defendant the opportunity to bid at the Sheriff's Sale. To do so would be the denial of the defendant's rights. The Sheriff's Sale should be conducted in a lawful manner that secures the best price for the property sold. *Note: The Sheriff is acting as an agent o the defendant in the raising of funds sufficient to satisfy the judgment. Absent specific instructions from the court, the Sheriff has total discretion in conducting the sale in order to bring in the best price. If this requires the auctioning off of the property one piece or item at a time, so be it.*

ILLEGAL SALE

The court can void and set aside a Sheriff's Sale in the event there was fraud, collusion, surprise or misleading statements in the conducting of the sale. Absent these acts, a grossly inadequate price is insufficient grounds for the setting aside of a Sheriff's Sale. The purchase of the property at auction by the plaintiff does not constitute an illegal sale. Neither would the purchase by the defendant.

Collusion to commit fraud could be penalized as a criminal act. Neither the Sheriff nor his deputies nor his employees are permitted to purchase at their own sale, nor should they procure anyone to do so on their behalf. (**O.C.G.A. 15-116-18**) To do so would constitute an illegal sale and the sale would be voided.

No attempt should be made to circumvent the laws governing judicial sales. An actual fraud or misrepresentation by the Sheriff or his deputy may bind the Sheriff personally.

The principle of vicarious liability binds the Sheriff for the acts committed by his deputies. The Sheriff may be found liable for contempt and may be fined, imprisoned, or removed from office in the manner prescribed by the Constitution and laws of the state of Georgia.

A purchaser at an illegal sale acquires no title to the property sold and may recover the purchase price paid the Sheriff under such illegal sale. A sale determined to be considered illegal will be declared void and no transfer of property permitted. Any further action will be at the discretion of the presiding judge.

POST SALE

SHERIFF'S DUTIES AFTER THE SALE

Following the sale, it is the responsibility of the Sheriff to prepare and provide a Sheriff's bill of sale at the purchaser's request. The Sheriff is entitled to charge a fee for this service as provided for by statute. These fees are nominal and are set by the legislature by statute.

Normally a bill of sale is mandated for vehicle, boats, trailers, real estate, etc. It was established practice at the author's agency to not charge for Sheriff's bills of sale for any of the aforementioned property, although entitled to these fees by statute.

Any other bills of sale would be at the request of the buyer and at the buyer's expense. For the purposes of documentation, it is recommended that a copy of all bills of sale issued be placed in the clerk's file for future reference.

A judicial sale is not exempt from the Sales Tax imposed by Georgia Law. A bidder claiming exemption from the Sales Tax should be required to present a copy of the applicable Sales Tax certificate prior to the sale. This copy should be retained in the permanent record of the sale. Real estate is exempt from Sales Tax as a matter of law.

Failure by the Sheriff to collect the Sales Tax makes the Sheriff liable for the Sales Tax personally. A failure to collect the Sales Tax is a misdemeanor and is punishable by not more that $100.00 or for imprisonment for up to three months in the county jail or both.

Failure to make a quarterly Sales Tax return to the **Georgia Department of Revenue** is a misdemeanor criminal offense and is punishable as such. The Sheriff or his deputies are not exempt from this requirement or its punishment.

SHERIFF'S FEES

O.C.G.A. 15-16-21B sets the fees that the Sheriff may charge for lawful services performed under the statutes. These fees imposed by statute very rarely ever off-set the actual expense incurred by the Sheriff in execution of these duties. In addition to fees for various other services, the Sheriff is entitled to fess for:

— each attempt at execution of writ of *Fi-Fa*

— entry of nulla bona

— commission from the proceeds of Sheriff's Sale

— for the issuance of a Sheriff's bill of sale

— execution of a writ of possession

— eviction

All <u>reasonable</u> fees, and expenses incurred in the collection of the judgment are recoverable before any proceeds of the judicial sale are applied to the principal. This may become an issue to be determined by the issuing judge as to what is *reasonable*.

Plaintiff should keep an accurate and detailed record of these expenses. Proper documentation will help to establish the reasonableness of the expenses and to ensure their recovery. The Sheriff's levy officer can apprise the plaintiff of the details.

APPLICATION OF
THE PROCEEDS

O.C.G.A. 9-13-60 says in part: (**c**) the proceeds of the Sheriff's Sale shall be applied first to;

(1) the payment of liens superior to the claims taken up by the plaintiff in execution,

(2) payment of principal advanced by the plaintiff in execution to put full legal title in defendant, with interest to the date of judicial sale.

(3) the balance to the execution under which the property was sold,

(4) then to other liens according to priority, to be determined as provided by law.

SATISFACTION OF THE JUDGMENT

"Knockdown" is to dispose of property to a bidder at an auction sale, hence the disposal of the property at a judicial or Sheriff's Sale *'knocks down'* the judgment by the amount netted or realized from the sale. This procedure involves the settling up of all the expenditures made by the plaintiff for advertising, towing, storage, etc., before the application of net proceeds to the judgment. This is limited to actual and reasonable expenses incurred by the plaintiff in the execution of the levy.

O.C.G.A. 9-13-80 requires that once the *Fi-Fa* has been satisfied, the plaintiff is required to direct the **Clerk of the Superior Court** to cancel the *Fi-Fa* upon the **G.E.D.** soonest. Once the judgment has been satisfied, the plaintiff is required to mark the *Fi-Fa* satisfied, then cancelled and cleared from the **G.E.D.**, and surrender it to the defendant.

O.C.G.A. 9-13-b (2) requires that this action to cancel be accomplished within 60 days of satisfaction of the judgment. **O.C.G.A. 9-13-80b (4)** states that the damages, or the penalty upon plaintiff, shall be presumed in the amount of $100.00 upon failure to comply. Actual damages may be recovered, but in no event shall recovery exceed $500.00.

Judgment plaintiff may elect to waive any or all post-judgment interest and/or fees incurred in collection, and/or any portion of the principal and consider the ***Fi-Fa*** satisfied, in return for sums or goods acceptable to the plaintiff. This is done everyday by the **I.R.S.** in settlement of Federal income tax ***Fi-Fa's***.

TOOLS FOR THE COLLECTION OF JUDGMENTS

RESOURCE MATERIALS

Some recommended resource materials for the collection of judgments:

— Black's Law Dictionary, 7th ed.

— Title 9, 15, &18 of the O.C.G.A.

— Georgia Post Judgment Collections with Forms, 4th ed. Stuart Finestone, West Group (formerly Harrison) available by telephoning 1 (800) 328 - 4880

— telephone directories for the relevant areas.

— local maps

— any relevant cross-reference directories

— a voter registration list

— a reliable computer with internet access

— subscription to a good credit reporting service

— resource file

A good reliable computer with substantial memory and a quality internet service provider (**I.S.P.**) prove invaluable. Through this medium you may access all sorts of research resources, with more being added all the time. Some counties and municipalities are already using their websites to post property transfers, voter registration lists, etc.

The **MSN** white pages and **AOL** white pages websites can help you locate the most current address and phone listing for your defendant. The information obtained should be printed out and retained to document the information and its source. Ultimately, it should be placed in the Clerk's permanent case file.

The **Secretary of State** website permits research into corporate entities. Corporate status, corporate officers, registered agent, addresses of the registered agent, etc., are all available. This is especially beneficial in the initial stages of the legal action in the matter of determining the proper style of the case and service of process.

To be enforceable, the writ must be properly styled and properly reflect the defendant named on the judgment. The Secretary of State website can very quickly become one of the most heavily used web addresses on your computer. MAPQUEST is another website that can be of invaluable assistance.

MAPS AND DIRECTORIES

Local and state maps, phone directories, voter registration lists and any available cross-reference directories, can be instrumental in attempting to '*skip-trace*' a defendant. Oftentimes local maps may be obtained from your local chamber of commerce or for a nominal fee from you r county planning office. State maps may be obtained free of charge from the nearest office of the **Georgia Department of Transportation**. Local telephone directories can be obtained free of charge from your phone company. Cross-reference directories are available at reasonable cost from the various publishers. Consult your local voter registrar for the fee amounts for obtaining a voter registration list. Some counties make these lists available on CD as well as a printed copy.

RESOURCE FILE

Create a resource file or directory. This can consist of any useful businesses, agencies or individuals that could be of assistance in providing reliable information or opinions relevant to the pursuit of judgment collection. Any source that was a help once may be needed again sometime in the future. Keep an amicable relationship with these sources. If you force them to cooperate on one occasion may deter them from being of service late.

List contact persons at credit bureaus, financial institutions, utilities, and sheriff's office levy officer, etc. You are limited only by what you find useful and wish to retain. This file can become absolutely indispensable over a period of time. If done on rotary file cards, you may add or discard as the need arises. Time tested sources are always at you fingertips for further research.

Keep a file on each judgment, retaining accurate and detailed notes and the documentation of efforts expended in the collection process and the expenses incurred. This may be comprised of receipts of recording fees, long distance phone calls, mileage accrued, etc.

This method has been found to be exceptionally helpful to finance companies, lending institutions, retail installment sales companies and rent-to-buy firms. It can be just as useful to an individual plaintiff. Legitimate, limited, reasonable costs incurred in the collection of the plaintiff's judgment are subject to recovery by the plaintiff.

There can never be enough emphasis placed on documentation. In some instances the author has encountered events that have resurfaced many years after the fact, requiring information from a levy and/or sale that might have been calamitous if not for the documentation. There is no substitute for hard facts, preserved through documentation and kept readily available for production as proof as required.

When documenting events, write or print legibly. Several months or years down the road someone may have to make a defense based on your notes and the author has seen officers that could not read their own handwriting after some time has passed.

Don't rely on half-measures. Details are very important. Success may hinge on the amount of effort expended. Make allowances to devote sufficient time to your endeavors. Rely on and have confidence in, the levy officer.

KEEPING THE JUDGMENT ALIVE

RERECORDING OF THE JUDGMENT

A judgment may become dormant seven years after it is rendered. Once it is dormant, it is no longer enforceable. To execute an unenforceable writ would be performing a wrongful levy.

Note: It is important that all steps be followed to keep the judgment alive. Georgia law is very specific in the steps and manner that a judgment is to be handled.

It is a very simple matter to keep the judgment alive and enforceable. The judgment *Fi-Fa* may be renewed by rerecording the writ on the **G.E.D.** within seven years of the issuance of the writ. To accomplish this, an entry of nulla bona must be made on the *Fi-Fa* by the Sheriff or another officer authorized to make levy and then taken to the **Clerk of Superior Court** of the county where issued and reentered on the **G.E.D.**

O.C.G.A. 9-12-60 (inclusive) prescribes the conditions and circumstances under which a judgment *Fi-Fa* may be rerecorded or otherwise become dormant. It is always best to attempt to not let the judgment reach this condition. In some instances this is difficult to prevent, for example, the inadvertent misplacing of the writ in a file, safety deposit box, etc. and forgetting about the location.

REVIVING THE JUDGMENT

Once a judgment does become dormant, it does not necessarily mean that all is irretrievably lost. There are some limited remedies available. The plaintiff should be cautioned to follow each and every step. Swift action should be taken to revive the judgment.

O.C.G.A. 9-12-61 provides that a dormant judgment may be revived and the procedures which must be followed. Within three years of the judgment becoming dormant a petition for **scire facias** may be filed to reopen the judgment. This is a new action and should be brought in the county where the defendant resides.

American National Bank v. Hodges 41 Ga.App. 717,154 S.E. 653(1930)

FORGIVING THE JUDGMENT

At any time the plaintiff feels that they have exhausted all available efforts at collection or the extent of their patience, they may forgive the judgment. The plaintiff can file the proper paperwork forgiving the debt and issuing an IRS form 1099-C to the defendant. This forces the defendant to have to report the debt to the IRS as income and pay the applicable state and federal income and F.I.C.A. taxes. The Internal Revenue Service should be able to advise as to the availability of the necessary forms.

USEFUL WEBSITES

The Official Code of Georgia is available at:

http://www.legis.state.ga.us

and then click on the box "GA Code" in the upper left of the screen.

Statistical release H. 15 at:

http://www.federalreserve.gov/releases/h15/update/

for obtaining the prime rate established by the Governors of the Federal Reserve System.

A free interest calculating program at:

http://www.pine-grove.com

And then downloading: 'Loan Calculator*Plus, Version 2.1'

Georgia Division of Motor Vehicle Services forms at:

http://www.dmvs.ga.gov/forms/motor.asp

Checking U.C.C. filings over the internet at:

http://www.gsccca.org/search/UCCC_Search/default.asp

BOUVIER LAW DICTIONARY, 6th ed. (1856) (online)

http://www.constitution.org/bouv/bouvier.htm

EVERYBODY'S LAW DICTIONARY, Nolo Press

http://www.nolo.com/lawcenter/dictionary/wordindex.cfm

The Georgia Department of Corrections:

http://www.dcor.state.ga.us/GDC/OffenderQuery/jsp/OffQryForm.jsp

Mapquest for mapping addresses of defendants and their property:

http://www.mapquest.com/

FORMS

A model for entry of levy on the writ of fieri facias (rubber stamp)

GEORGIA, Any county

I have this the _____ day of _____, 20 _____

Levied on the following property to wit;

_____
_____
_____
_____
_____
_____
_____
_____

Said property found to be in the possession of

_____ ,

the defendant in Fi-Fa and owning _____ per cent undivided interest in same.

_____

Deputy Sheriff

A model for entry of nulla bona (rubber stamp)

GEORGIA, Any county

After due and diligent search I have been unable to find any property belonging to the defendant in said county.

This the _____ day of _____ 20 _____

_____

Deputy Sheriff

A model entry of "knock down" (rubber stamp)

GEORGIA, Any County

I have this the _____ day of _____, 20 _____

conducted a Sheriff's Sale in and for said county, with the highest bidder

Being; _____ and said sale having brought

$ _____

After deducting the following;

Sheriff's commission $_____

Towing, storage, etc. $_____

Other lawfully

recoverable costs $_____ (itemized)

Net proceeds were $_____

Said net proceeds to be applied toward the principal amount.

_____

Deputy Sheriff

A model Fi-Fa collection letter

John Law
Sheriff
Any County, Georgia
P.O. Box 123
Anytown, GA

August 9, 2005

Mr. John N. Dough   K. T. Killjoy, D.D.S.
4321 Oak Street S.W.   v.
Anytown, GA 12345   John N. Dough

Dear Mr. Dough,

There has been placed in my hands for collection, a judgment in the above styled case in the amount of _____, plus interest and costs. I can hold this matter in abeyance for Ten (10) days. Please contact me at your earliest convenience to discuss this matter.

After such time further action will be taken to make levy or alternative methods of collection. I will be awaiting your timely response.

Respectfully,

_____
Deputy Sheriff

A model for a Sheriff's Sale legal advertisement:

Legal advertisement to be published: _____

_____

_____

Sheriff's Sale

Georgia, Any County

There will be sold at public outcry, to the highest and best bidder for cash, between the legal hours of sale,before the Any County court house, 1234 Main Street S.W., Anytown, in Any County, Georgia on the first Tuesday in _____ _____ next and each day thereafter until sold. The following described property to wit:

Said property found in possession of _____ _____. And owning one hundred per cent undivided interest. Levied on to satisfy an execution in favor of _____ plaintiff against _____ defendant, issued from the _____ court of _____, Georgia as the property of the defendant in Fi-Fa. Notice of levy and sale having been given the defendant in Fi-Fa.

This the _____ day of _____ , 20 _____

John Law, Sheriff, Any County, GA

_____

By Deputy Sheriff

A model for notice of levy and sale:

NOTICE OF LEVY AND SALE

Georgia, Any County

To _____
owner of certain property located at _____
_____ in Any County, Georgia, described
as:

     You are hereby notified that I have this day levied a Fi-Fa,
issued from the_____ Court of _____
_____ , Georgia, in favor of_____
_____ plaintiff, against _____
Defendant (s), owner (s) of the aforesaid property. You are
further notified that said property will be sold on the first
Tuesday in _____, next.

This the _____day of _____, 20 _____

John Law, Sheriff

_____
Deputy Sheriff, Any County, GA

A model for a Fi-Fa collection procedures flyer for public distribution

FI-FA COLLECTION PROCEDURES

19-13-10 O.C.G.A. (Official Code of Georgia Annotated) requires the Sheriff (or his lawful deputy) to make levies pursuant to a writ of fieri facias (*Fi-Fa*) or other writ of attachment on the property, either real or personal or both, of the defendant in *Fi-Fa*. Plaintiff must first have received a monetary judgment from the court before a writ of *Fi-Fa* may be issued. When the *Fi-Fa* has been recorded on the **General Execution Docket** (G.E.D.), it should be taken to the sheriff's office civil section for action by the levy officer. If the defendant has property in another county, the *Fi-Fa* should be entered on the **G.E.D.** of that county and then taken to the sheriff of the respective county for action.

Plaintiff may pursue a garnishment of the defendant's employer and/or bank account **(O.C.G.A. 18-4-64)** while simultaneously attempting a levy under *Fi-Fa*. If the plaintiff is not familiar with the defendant's place of employment, bank accounts, or property owned, defendant may be served with post-judgment interrogatories in an attempt to obtain this information. Interrogatories are a set of questions whereby the defendant must list any assets, both real and personal, and file back with the court under penalty of contempt.

Upon receiving a *Fi-Fa*, it has been our established policy to mail the defendant a '*Fi-Fa* collection letter' in hopes that the defendant will voluntarily respond to resolve the judgment. This step is not required by law, but does produce some noticeable results.

It is the responsibility of the plaintiff to locate any property of the defendant that is not subject to any prior outstanding lien. In the case of motor vehicles, **O.C.G.A. 40-2-130(c)** requires and authorizes any officer to ascertain any outstanding liens for the judgment creditor. Plaintiff must be careful not to over-levy and run the risk of being subject to possible litigation by the defendant. Plaintiff should also note that if the levied property does not produce sufficient proceeds at Sheriff's Sale to offset the costs incurred, plaintiff is responsible for the difference.

When approaching defendant for collection, the levy officer first makes oral demand for payment. If payment is not made, defendant is permitted by law **(9-13-50(a) O.C.G.A.)** to designate the property upon which to levy that would be sufficient to satisfy the judgment *Fi-Fa*. Failing this response, it is the responsibility of the plaintiff to designate the property upon which to levy. **Title 44 chapter 13 O.C.G.A**. provides for constitutional and statutory **exemption**s from levy.

The property must be published in a **Notice of Sheriff's Sale** in the legal organ of the county for the four weeks immediately prior to sale and sold at public auction the first Tuesday in the month following publication. **15-16-10(a)(4) O.C.G.A.** requires the Sheriff to maintain bound copies of the newspaper selected as legal organ in the same manner as required by law for the **Clerk of Superior Court.** The time of the sale is set pursuant to **9-13-160 O.C.G.A.** The costs of legal advertisement are due and payable in advance by the plaintiff.

Arrangement for and payment of any towing, transport, storage, etc., are the responsibility of the plaintiff. Storage must be safe, secure and inside the county where seized (preferably in a bonded and insured warehouse). Plaintiff is entitled to recover any reasonable costs incurred in the collection of the payment from the proceeds of the sale. These costs should be documented. The **Fi-Fa** is in force for seven years and is renewable every seven years thereafter. If the full amount of the judgment is not realized from the initial levy, additional levies can be made until the judgment is satisfied.

GLOSSARY OF TERMS

Action – a statement of claim, a lawsuit.

Adjudication - (a): a judicial decision or sentence from a court action, (b): a decree in a bankruptcy.

Affidavit - a written statement, made under sworn oath, giving facts pertinent to the case in question.

Allegation - complaint or claim made against the defendant.

Answer – the response admitting or denying the claim or complaint.

Appeal - the judicial process where a judicial decision or judgment is referred to a higher court for reconsideration of the merits of the case or other issues that may overturn the decision.

Asset - **1.** : An item of value owned. **2.:** Property of a person, association, corporation, or estate applicable or subject to the payment of debts.

Case law - where a case has been appealed to a higher court and a decision has been rendered either affirming or denying judgment setting a precedent whereby future decisions will be judged.

Caveat – **1** : a cautionary warning, **2:** a legal warning to a judicial officer to suspend a proceeding.

Circumstantial evidence - the situation, conditions or circumstances surrounding the issue

Common law - judicial decisions based on early English law before legislatures were operational.

Complaint - The legal method used to present the plaintiff's grounds (grievance) for suit against the defendant for consideration by the court, the complaint outlines the debt or particular wrong for which the plaintiff is seeking redress.

Consent judgment - an agreement that has been consented to by both the plaintiff and defendant jointly stating the conditions by which the issue has been resolved. Once signed by the judge, it is as binding as a judicial decision rendered after trial.

Default judgment - summary judgment rendered by the court when the defendant, after having been duly served, fails to properly respond to the action.

Deposition - statements made under oath, taken down at a time other than during court that under certain circumstances may be placed into evidence for consideration by the court.

Discovery – the process by which information regarding the issue at hand may be obtained.

Dismissal - termination of civil action due to lack of merit, evidence, improper venue, etc.

Disposition - the results of the judicial proceedings. More commonly called the judgment.

Domestication - the legal process whereby the merits and validity of a judgment rendered by a court in another state is determined before a Fi-Fa is issued for execution locally.

Dormant judgment – a judgment that is older than seven years and has not been rerecorded.

Due process - procedures established pursuant to the Fourteenth Amendment to the Constitution guarantees that no one shall be deprived of life, liberty, or property without *due process.*

Duty – a lawful obligation, a legal responsibility

Evidence - facts placed before the courts through various methods.

Execution – verb; act of carrying into effect the final judgment of a court or other jurisdiction, in fact, the process of enforcing a legal judgment (*as against a debtor*), noun; the judicial writ which authorizes the officer to carry into effect such judgment is also called an execution.

Extraordinary writ - A writ, often issued by an appellate court, making available remedies not regularly within the powers of lower courts.

Fieri facias (fi ree fay shious) - *noun:* a writ authorizing the sheriff to obtain satisfaction of a judgment in debt or damages from the goods and chattels of the defendant in Fi-Fa. From the Latin, cause it to be done.

Garnishment - a civil action filed with the court that orders an employer, financial institution, or others holding funds due the defendant to be withheld and paid into the coffers of the court for disbursement to the plaintiff.

General Execution Docket - Official register maintained by the Clerk of Superior Court of the county for the recordation of liens, judgments and writs of execution.

Interrogatories – a set of written questions served on either party in a case upon their adversary to obtain or discover additional information about the case at hand.

Judicial sale – the transfer of property at auction pursuant to an order of the court.

Judgment - a formal decision given by a court putting the issue to rest (a): an obligation (as a debt) created by the decree of a court (b): a certificate giving evidence of such a decree; a writ.

Jurisdiction - the legal authority of the particular court to decide the issue in question.

Knockdown - to dispose of property to a bidder at an auction sale, the disposal of property at a judicial or Sheriff's sale '*knocks down*' the judgment by the amount netted or realized from the sale.

Levy - 1) *noun:* the imposition or collection of an assessment or judgment. - 2) *verb:* to impose or collect by legal authority <as levy a tax>.

Lien - 1): a claim charge upon real or personal property for the satisfaction of some debt or duty ordinarily arising by operation of law. 2): the security interest created by a mortgage.

Malfeasance - intentional wrongdoing or misconduct, particularly by a public official.

Misfeasance - the performance of a lawful action in an illegal or improper manner, most often alleged against a public official.

Mediation - alternative to court proceeding where the parties attempt to reach a solution or agreement on their own without the intervention of a judge. A trained and impartial mediator oversees the discussion and helps the parties come to a workable settlement of decision. This requires some degree of willingness to compromise on the part of both parties.

Nonfeasance - a failure to act; especially: a knowing failure to do what ought to be done, particularly by a public official.

Official Code of Georgia Annotated - the official codification of the constitution, laws and statutes of the state of Georgia.

Party – either plaintiff or defendant in the particular action.

Perjury – the act of knowingly making a false statement after first having been administered an oath or affirmation to tell the truth.

Physical evidence - actual items that can be shown to the court for consideration.

Presumption – a conclusion drawn from the proven facts and issues in evidence.

Property -: (a) real: real estate, (b) personal: any property other than real estate.

Punitive damages - damages levied, exacted, or rendered by a civil court or civil jury as a punishment against the defendant for wrongful actions.

Recovery - a recovery, in its most extensive sense, is the restoration of a former right, by the solemn judgment of a Court of justice, extending to the reimbursement for expenditures made and expenses incurred, in the pursuit of the judgment.

Redress - the act of receiving satisfaction for an injury sustained.

Rejoinder - the name of the defendant's answer or pleadings to the plaintiff's complaint.

Replevin – a civil action for the recovery of a possession that has been wrongfully taken or seized.

Replevy (replevin) bond - bond posted by the defendant allowing the return of the property pending a hearing on the propriety or legality of the levy, also called a supersedeas bond or forthcoming bond.

Respondent - the person against whom the allegations or complaint are filed, more commonly referred to as the defendant.

Reversal - upon appeal, a decision by a higher court overturning or reversing the decision obtained from the lower court.

Subpoena - the legal method used to summon witnesses to come to testify in court on the issue at hand.

Stay of Execution – an order issued by the court suspending the levy or Sheriff's sale pending further order of the court.

Subpoena duces tecum - a subpoena used to require the production of documents, records or other evidence crucial to the issue before the court.

Summons - the legal medium by which the court requires the defendant to respond to the complaint filed by the plaintiff.

Testimonial evidence - testimony or statements made under oath by witnesses in the court room for consideration by the court.

Trespass – to enter the property of another without authority.

Venue - the determination of the proper forum for the hearing of the action. That the action is filed in the proper court of authority or jurisdiction.

Vicarious liability - the legal theory whereby responsibility extends upward to the highest level of knowledge, actual or by the duty or obligation to know.

Void – without legal force or effect, legally nonexistent.

Waiver - the decision of a defendant, lien-holder, etc., to relinquish or give up specific legal rights under law.

Writ - A precept issued by the court of authority, and in the name of the sovereign or the state, for the purpose of compelling the defendant to do something therein designated, enforced by the Sheriff.

Writ of execution - A writ to put in force the decision or judgment, that the court has rendered; it is addressed to the Sheriff commanding him, relative to the nature of the case, either to give the plaintiff possession of lands; or to enforce the delivery of a chattel which was the subject of the action; or to execute levy for the plaintiff.

ABOUT THE AUTHOR

The author is a native and lifelong resident of Hall County, Georgia. He was educated in Gainesville and Hall County public schools. Rickey is married to the former Florence Patricia Turk Hand, a 1988 graduate of Brenau University, the Professional College, receiving a B.S. degree with majors in both Criminal Justice and Public Administration, and graduated with honors. A Georgia P.O.S.T. certified, career veteran of more than 32 years with the Hall County Sheriff's Office, having attended and successfully completed the required mandate training at the Georgia Police Academy in Atlanta, GA. Having retired from a career of more than 32 years with the Hall County Georgia Sheriff's Office with service spanning over three years as a jailer, more than 11 years on road patrol and over 18 years as a Court Services Officer, gaining direct hands on experience with civil process, writs and other attachments and has held supervisory positions in three Divisions within the Hall County Sheriff's Office. He is now operating his own business; CIVIL PROCESS SERVERS OF NORTHEAST GEORGIA providing free-lance services as a special process server to the attorneys in the area. The web address of Civil Process Servers of Northeast Georgia is;

http://hometown.aol.com/civilprocess1/civilprocessservers.html

NOTES